MAD ABOUT
MACARONI

RODALE
TEST KITCHEN

RODALE'S
New.
Classics™

MAD ABOUT
MACARONI

By Anne Egan

RODALE

Rodale's New Classics and Favorite Recipes Made Easy for Today's Lifestyle are trademarks of Rodale Inc.

Printed in China.

Cover and Interior Designer: Richard Kershner

Cover and Interior Photos: Rodale Images

Front Cover Recipe: Rigatoni Alfredo (page 11)

Library of Congress Cataloging-in-Publication Data

Egan, Anne.

  Mad about macaroni / by Anne Egan.

      p.   cm. — (Rodale's new classics)

    ISBN 1–57954–343–X paperback

    1. Cookery (Pasta). 2. Pasta products. I. Title.

  TX809.M17 .E33 2001

  641.8'22—dc21   00–010430

Distributed to the book trade by St. Martin's Press

2 4 6 8 10 9 7 5 3 1   paperback

Visit us on the Web at www.rodalecookbooks.com, or call us toll-free at (800) 848-4735.

WE **INSPIRE** AND **ENABLE** PEOPLE TO IMPROVE
THEIR LIVES AND THE WORLD AROUND THEM

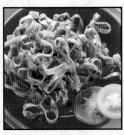

**FETTUCCINE
WITH
GORGONZOLA
PESTO**
Page 22

**SOUTHWESTERN
CHICKEN
LASAGNA**
Page 67

Contents

**FETTUCCINE
SHRIMP
PRIMAVERA**
Page 93

**PENNE
WITH SPRING
VEGETABLES**
Page 109

Introduction

Macaroni was my first introduction to the world of pasta. When I was growing up in the 1960s, most pasta dishes—regardless of the pasta used—were called macaroni. The most popular ones were spaghetti and meatballs and macaroni and cheese. As my culinary awareness grew, so did the pasta products that were readily accessible. Today, more varieties than ever, both fresh and dried, are available to help us get exciting dinners on the table.

Technically, macaroni is the name for tubular pastas as well as shells, twists, and other short shapes. Many Italian Americans still refer to pasta as macaroni and that, plus my earliest memories of pasta, was the inspiration for this book. Titled *Mad about Macaroni*, this book is actually filled with recipes using all types of pasta (spaghetti, macaroni, stuffed) and noodles.

Although a pasta dinner can be as simple as pouring a bottled sauce over a bowl of noodles, preparing a complete, wholesome dinner for your family can be almost as easy. Here's how to prepare delicious, good-for-you recipes that are sure to please even the pickiest eater while ensuring your family's well-being. It's really quite simple.

In *Rodale's New Classics*, I show you how to enjoy the process of cooking while feeling confident that you are feeding your family the best foods. This is achieved by using the fastest possible ingredients and cooking techniques. Many of the sauce recipes in this book are ready by the time the pasta has cooked, such as the Linguine with Fresh Puttanesca Sauce. Others, like my New Classic Beef Lasagna, take just minutes in the kitchen and then can be left to bake while you are off enjoying your family.

Cooking Basics

Almost everyone can cook pasta with acceptable results, but for the best-cooked noodle every time, follow these simple steps.

The key to perfectly cooked pasta—without a sticky mess—is to cook it in plenty of water. Use 4 to 6 quarts of water per 1 pound of pasta. When the water has come to a boil, stir in the pasta and salt and return the water to a boil.

Give the pasta a stir occasionally during cooking. Be sure to keep an eye on the cooking time. It is best to follow the time suggested on the package, but start checking for doneness about 4 minutes before the final cook time. Times will always vary, and checking early will ensure that it is properly cooked.

If the pasta requires additional cooking, such as in a casserole, undercook the pasta a bit so that it doesn't become too soft in the final dish.

The key to perfect-tasting

pasta—with plenty of flavor—is to add salt to the water. One table-spoon of salt should be added to the water with the pasta. (The pasta will take on only a fraction of the salt.) This will enhance the flavor of the pasta as well as help it absorb the sauce.

The key to the perfect texture—without a mushy consistency—is to cook it until *al dente*. Meaning "to the tooth" in Italian, al dente pasta should be firm to the bite yet cooked through. Be sure to drain the pasta immediately and then toss it with the sauce once drained. If you are not going to sauce it right away, then add 1 teaspoon of olive oil to keep it from sticking.

Pasta should be rinsed only if it is to be used in a cold dish. For these dishes, a quick rinse under cold running water will stop the cooking process.

Shapes

Half of the fun of cooking pasta is choosing which

shape to use. Today, supermarket shelves are filled with an abundance of options. Follow these basic principles to make the best choice every time.

Long pasta, such as spaghetti, linguine, and angel hair, is eaten twirled on a fork. Light, thin sauces, such as tomato or olive oil, are best so that the sauce will cling to the pasta when twirled.

Thick-strand pasta, such as fettuccine and pappardelle, has a porous texture that absorbs rich sauces. Butter- and cream-based ones are best for thick pasta.

Short, tubular macaroni, such as penne, shells, and radiatore, works well with chunky meat and vegetable sauces. The cavities of these shapes are great for holding the bits of a chunky sauce.

Tiny shapes, such as acini di peppe, orzo, and ditalini, work well in soups, salads, and side dishes.

Stuffed pasta, such as tortellini, ravioli, and agnolotti, is delicious with a mild sauce. Be sure to go easy on the sauce so that the flavor of the filling is not overpowered.

Sauces

While the large assortment of pasta shapes can add variety to a dish, it's the sauce that distinguishes one meal from the next. Feel free to experiment with the sauces here. For example, if the vegetables called for in the recipe are not in season, switch to ones that are. If you have an abundance of an herb, use it instead of the one called for.

When preparing the sauce, you may notice that it seems to need a touch of liquid. Adding a bit of the pasta water will loosen the sauce while adding a hint of the pasta flavor. I always reserve about 1 cup of the water before draining the pasta. When the sauce and pasta are tossed together, I add some of the water to reach the best consistency.

Whether you call it macaroni, pasta, or noodles, everyone has a passion for it. No other food can beat pasta for its versatility. Dressed in anything from a drizzle of olive oil to a cheesy cream sauce, there is a pasta dish that is sure to please the entire family. All you'll need is a simple salad to round out any of these recipes into a lovely meal. Enjoy!

PLENTIFUL MEATLESS DISHES

Rigatoni Alfredo

12 ounces rigatoni

1 cup milk

½ cup (4 ounces) sour cream

2 cloves garlic, minced

½ teaspoon freshly ground nutmeg

½ teaspoon salt

½ teaspoon freshly ground black pepper

⅔ cup (2½ ounces) shredded Parmesan cheese

½ cup walnuts, toasted and coarsely chopped

¼ cup thinly sliced fresh basil

This simple cream sauce, bursting with basil and Parmesan cheese, makes an elegant dinner that's ready in minutes. For a change of pace, substitute pecans and Asiago for the walnuts and Parmesan.

Prepare the rigatoni according to package directions. Drain and return to the pot.

Stir in the milk, sour cream, garlic, nutmeg, salt, pepper, and ⅓ cup of the cheese and cook over low heat, stirring constantly, for 3 minutes, or until thick and bubbling.

Add the walnuts and basil. Toss to combine. Place in a serving bowl and top with the remaining ⅓ cup cheese.

Makes 6 servings

Per serving: 381 calories, 14 g protein, 48 g carbohydrates, 14 g fat, 21 mg cholesterol, 1 g fiber, 427 mg sodium

Cheesy Baked Penne

12 ounces penne

1 tablespoon olive oil

1 large onion, chopped

¼ cup chopped dry-packed sun-dried tomatoes

2 cloves garlic, minced

2 cans (15 ounces each) stewed tomatoes

¼ cup vermouth or white wine

3 tablespoons chopped fresh basil

10 large kalamata olives, pitted and sliced

¼ cup (1 ounce) grated Parmesan cheese

1 cup (4 ounces) shredded mozzarella cheese

Sun-dried tomatoes offer a nice flavor to this simple baked pasta dish. You can make the sauce up to 2 days ahead and refrigerate it. Then, just mix in the cooked pasta and pop it in the oven for a quick meal.

Preheat the oven to 350°F. Coat a 2½ quart baking dish with cooking spray.

Prepare the penne according to package directions.

Meanwhile, heat the oil in a large saucepan over medium heat. Add the onion and sun-dried tomatoes and cook for 5 minutes, or until the onion is soft. Add the garlic and cook for 2 minutes. Stir in the stewed tomatoes (with juice), wine, and basil. Simmer, stirring occasionally, for 5 minutes.

Stir in the cooked penne, olives, Parmesan, and ½ cup of the mozzarella. Place in the prepared dish. Sprinkle with the remaining ½ cup mozzarella.

Bake for 20 minutes, or until hot and bubbly.

Makes 4 servings

Per serving: 578 calories, 21 g protein, 86 g carbohydrates, 15 g fat, 27 mg cholesterol, 4 g fiber, 874 mg sodium

Bow Ties with Greens

8 ounces bow-tie pasta (farfalle)

2 tablespoons olive oil

¼ cup chopped oil-packed sun-dried tomatoes

1 small onion, chopped

2 cloves garlic, minced

5 cups chopped assorted fresh bitter greens (such as arugula, mustard, watercress, dandelion greens)

¼ cup white wine or vegetable broth

½ teaspoon lemon peel

½ teaspoon salt

¼ cup (1 ounce) shredded Asiago cheese

¼ cup pine nuts, toasted

Bitter greens are slightly mellowed when wilted in this flavor-packed dish.

Prepare the bow ties according to package directions.

Meanwhile, heat the oil in a large skillet over medium-high heat. Add the tomatoes, onion, and garlic and cook for 5 minutes, or until soft. Add the greens and cook for 1 minute. Add the wine or broth and cook for 1 minute, or until the greens are wilted. Season with the lemon peel and salt.

Place the bow ties in a large bowl and toss with the greens mixture. Top with the cheese and nuts.

Makes 4 servings

Per serving: 370 calories, 13 g protein, 49 g carbohydrates, 14 g fat, 5 mg cholesterol, 3 g fiber, 488 mg sodium

Spicy Shells

8 ounces small shells
2 tablespoons olive oil
2 cloves garlic, minced
1 can (14 ounces) Italian-style chopped tomatoes
½ cup vegetable broth
1 tablespoon Italian seasoning
¼ teaspoon crushed red-pepper flakes
½ teaspoon salt
1 can (14–19 ounces) chickpeas, rinsed and drained

Keep your pantry stocked with these ingredients, and you will have a nutritious dinner at your fingertips.

Prepare the shells according to package directions.

Meanwhile, heat the oil in a large skillet over medium-high heat. Add the garlic and cook for 1 minute. Add the tomatoes (with juice), broth, Italian seasoning, red-pepper flakes, and salt.

Bring to a boil over high heat. Reduce the heat to low, cover, and simmer for 4 minutes. Add the chickpeas and cook for 2 minutes, or until heated through.

Place the shells in a serving bowl and top with the sauce.

Makes 4 servings

Per serving: 481 calories, 17 g protein, 79 g carbohydrates, 12 g fat, 0 mg cholesterol, 8 g fiber, 760 mg sodium

Shells with Tarragon-Mushroom Sauce

8 ounces medium shells
2 tablespoons olive oil
4 shallots, thinly sliced
3 cloves garlic, minced
16 ounces portobello mushrooms, chopped
½ teaspoon salt
½ teaspoon freshly ground black pepper
1 cup vegetable broth
¼ cup dry white wine or sherry
2 ounces goat cheese, crumbled
1 tablespoon fresh tarragon

Flavorful goat cheese adds creaminess to this mushroom sauce. If you prefer a milder cheese, brie makes a nice substitute.

Prepare the shells according to package directions.

Meanwhile, heat the oil in a large saucepan over medium-high heat. Add the shallots and garlic and cook for 4 minutes, or until the shallots are soft. Stir in the mushrooms, salt, and pepper and cook for 5 minutes, or until the mushrooms release their juices.

Add the broth and wine. Bring to a boil over high heat. Reduce the heat to low and simmer, uncovered, for 5 minutes to blend the flavors. Stir in the cheese and tarragon and cook for 2 minutes, or until the cheese is melted.

Place the shells in a serving bowl and top with the mushroom sauce.

Makes 4 servings
Per serving: 383 calories, 16 g protein, 50 g carbohydrates, 12 g fat, 11 mg cholesterol, 5 g fiber, 257 mg sodium

---

COOKING TIP

Feel free to use a variety of mushrooms for the portobellos. A mixture of porcini, shiitake, and morels works nicely as do simple button mushrooms.

Linguine with Fresh Puttanesca Sauce

8   ounces linguine
1   tablespoon butter
1   onion, chopped
4   large tomatoes, chopped
½   cup chopped fresh basil
4   cloves garlic, minced
1   tablespoon chopped oil-packed sun-dried tomatoes
10   kalamata olives, pitted and sliced

Perfect for a last-minute summer supper—this fresh tomato sauce is ready in minutes. For a richer dish, top with grated fresh Parmesan cheese.

Prepare the linguine according to package directions.

Melt the butter in a large skillet over medium heat. Add the onion and cook, stirring occasionally, for 2 minutes. Add the tomatoes, basil, garlic, sun-dried tomatoes, and olives and cook for 5 minutes to blend the flavors.

Place the linguine in a serving bowl. Top with the sauce.

Makes 4 servings

Per serving: 344 calories, 12 g protein, 40 g carbohydrates, 16 g fat, 15 mg cholesterol, 4 g fiber, 418 mg sodium

Cheesy Macaroni and Cauliflower

8   ounces elbow macaroni
2   tablespoons butter
3   tablespoons all-purpose flour
3   cups low-fat milk
1   can (14½ ounces) diced tomatoes, drained
1   package (10 ounces) frozen cauliflower florets, thawed
1   cup (4 ounces) shredded fontina cheese
¼   teaspoon mustard powder
¾   cup (3 ounces) grated Asiago cheese
3   tablespoons seasoned dry bread crumbs

Here is the perfect way to sneak vegetables into your family's meals. The rich, creamy taste of the baked macaroni is the perfect disguise for the tender cauliflower. They'll never know it's hiding in there.

Preheat the oven to 375°F. Coat a 2½ quart baking dish with cooking spray.

Prepare the macaroni according to package directions.

Meanwhile, melt the butter in a large saucepan over medium heat. Stir in the flour and cook, stirring, for 1 minute, or until the flour is lightly browned. Stir in the milk until smooth. Cook, stirring often, for 8 minutes, or until thickened. Remove from the heat and stir in the tomatoes (with juice), cauliflower, fontina, mustard powder, and ½ cup of the Asiago. Add the cooked macaroni and toss to coat well. Place in the prepared baking dish. Top with the bread crumbs and the remaining ¼ cup Asiago.

Bake for 30 minutes, or until hot and bubbly.

Makes 6 servings
Per serving: 407 calories, 21 g protein, 44 g carbohydrates, 16 g fat, 47 mg cholesterol, 3 g fiber, 866 mg sodium

COOKING TIP

To boost the nutrition of this dish even more, use whole wheat elbow macaroni.

Gnocchi in Creamy Herbed Sauce

1   **package (16 ounces) frozen gnocchi**

2   **tablespoons butter**

¼   **cup finely chopped shallots**

2   **tablespoons chopped fresh sage or 1½ teaspoons rubbed sage**

½   **cup dry white wine**

½   **cup half-and-half or milk**

2   **tablespoons grated Parmesan cheese**

½   **teaspoon salt**

½   **teaspoon freshly ground black pepper**

2   **tablespoons chopped toasted pecans**

Gnocchi is a pasta made with a potato dough, so it has a hearty, toothy bite. Available in the freezer section of your supermarket, look for spinach gnocchi, too.

Prepare the gnocchi according to package directions.

Meanwhile, melt the butter in a medium saucepan over medium-high heat. Add the shallots and sage and cook, stirring, for 2 minutes. Stir in the wine and heat for 30 seconds. Remove the saucepan from the heat. Add the half-and-half and cheese. Cook over medium heat for 4 minutes, or until the sauce reduces by about one-third. Season with the salt and pepper. Place the gnocchi in a serving bowl. Top with the sauce and pecans.

Makes 4 servings

Per serving: 250 calories, 7 g protein, 35 g carbohydrates, 8 g fat, 21 mg cholesterol, 2 g fiber, 610 mg sodium

---

COOKING TIP

The step of adding the heated wine to the half-and-half tempers the half-and-half and keeps it from breaking, or separating, to give you a smooth, creamy sauce.

Fettuccine with Gorgonzola Pesto

12 ounces tomato fettuccine

6 cups packed basil leaves

¼ cup (1 ounce) grated Romano cheese

½ cup (2 ounces) crumbled Gorgonzola cheese

¼ cup pine nuts, toasted

¼ cup olive oil

3 cloves garlic

½ teaspoon salt

1 teaspoon freshly ground black pepper

Gorgonzola and basil blend together so nicely, this quick dish is sure to become a favorite—especially in summer when fresh basil is plentiful.

Prepare the fettuccine according to package directions.

Meanwhile, to make the pesto, combine the basil, Romano, Gorgonzola, pine nuts, oil, garlic, salt, and pepper in a food processor or blender. Process until smooth.

Place the fettuccine in a serving bowl. Toss with the pesto.

Makes 6 servings
Per serving: 338 calories, 13 g protein, 34 g carbohydrates, 18 g fat, 72 mg cholesterol, 3 g fiber, 331 mg sodium

Southwest Corn Salsa over Angel Hair

12 ounces angel hair pasta
½ cup vegetable broth
5 tablespoons lime juice
5 tablespoons olive oil
1 chipotle chile pepper in adobo sauce
1 large tomato, chopped
½ cup frozen corn, thawed
1 avocado, chopped
¼ cup chopped fresh cilantro
2 cloves garlic, minced
1 small red onion, minced

Summer-fresh vegetables make a zesty sauce for tossing with angel hair pasta. Perfect for last-minute dining, this meal comes together in minutes.

Prepare the angel hair according to package directions.

Meanwhile, in a blender or food processor, combine the broth, 4 tablespoons of the lime juice, 4 tablespoons of the oil, and the chipotle pepper. Process until smooth.

In a bowl, combine the tomato, corn, avocado, cilantro, garlic, onion, the remaining 1 tablespoon lime juice, and the remaining 1 tablespoon oil.

Place the pasta in a serving bowl and toss with the chipotle mixture. Top with the salsa.

Makes 4 servings
Per serving: 535 calories, 13 g protein, 61 g carbohydrates, 29 g fat, 95 mg cholesterol, 6 g fiber, 127 mg sodium

COOKING TIP

Look for canned chipotle chile peppers in the ethnic aisle in your supermarket. Store any remaining chipotles in a tightly covered container in the refrigerator for up to 1 month. Their smoky flavor will add zing to your next batch of chili or fajitas.

Easy Spinach Manicotti

1 jar (26 ounces) tomato-herb pasta sauce

12 manicotti shells

1 container (15 ounces) ricotta cheese

1 package (10 ounces) frozen chopped spinach, thawed and squeezed dry

1 cup (4 ounces) shredded mozzarella cheese

¼ cup (1 ounce) grated Parmesan cheese

2 eggs

2 teaspoons fennel seed, crushed

This simple supper goes together in minutes. It is a perfect dish to make ahead—just cover and refrigerate until ready to bake. Add an extra 10 minutes if it goes into the oven cold.

Preheat the oven to 350°F. Spray a 13" x 9" baking dish with cooking spray. Spread ¾ cup of the sauce over the bottom of the prepared pan.

Prepare the manicotti according to package directions.

Meanwhile, in a large bowl, combine the ricotta, spinach, mozzarella, Parmesan, eggs, and fennel seed. Evenly divide the cheese mixture among the manicotti. Place in a single layer in the prepared baking dish and top with the remaining sauce.

Cover with foil and bake for 20 minutes. Remove the foil and bake for 5 minutes, or until hot and bubbly.

Makes 6 servings

Per serving: 390 calories, 23 g protein, 39 g carbohydrates, 17 g fat, 125 mg cholesterol, 4 g fiber, 742 mg sodium

COOKING TIP

The fastest way to fill manicotti shells is to use a pastry bag and pipe the filling into the shells. If you don't have a pastry bag, use a resealable plastic bag that has had one corner snipped off.

Squash-Stuffed Shells

1 jar (26 ounces) chunky pasta sauce

24 jumbo shells

1 package (12 ounces) frozen squash puree, thawed

¾ cup (6 ounces) ricotta cheese

⅓ cup (1½ ounces) grated Asiago cheese

1 egg, lightly beaten

2 tablespoons dry seasoned bread crumbs

1 teaspoon freshly ground nutmeg

Creamy squash blends deliciously with this cheesy filling for a new twist on stuffed shells. For an autumn treat, substitute canned pumpkin for the squash.

Preheat the oven to 350°F. Coat a 13" x 9" baking dish with cooking spray. Spread half of the sauce over the bottom of the prepared baking dish.

Prepare the shells according to package directions.

Meanwhile, in a medium bowl, combine the squash, ricotta, Asiago, egg, bread crumbs, and nutmeg.

Evenly divide the squash mixture among the shells. Arrange in a single layer in the prepared baking dish. Pour the remaining sauce over the filled shells. Cover with foil and bake for 20 minutes. Remove the foil and bake for 5 minutes, or until hot and bubbly.

Makes 8 servings

Per serving: 231 calories, 10 g protein, 32 g carbohydrates, 6 g fat, 42 mg cholesterol, 3 g fiber, 474 mg sodium

Ravioli with Lemon-Chive Sauce

1 package (16 ounces) frozen mushroom or cheese ravioli
2 teaspoons olive oil
1 shallot, finely chopped
2 teaspoons flour
1 cup milk
½ cup (4 ounces) sour cream
¼ cup chopped fresh chives
1 tablespoon lemon juice
½ teaspoon salt
½ teaspoon freshly ground black pepper
1 teaspoon shredded lemon peel
½ cup (2 ounces) grated Romano cheese

Bursting with fresh lemon and chive flavors, this sauce is lovely atop tender ravioli.

Prepare the ravioli according to package directions.

Meanwhile, heat the oil in a small saucepan over medium heat. Add the shallot and cook for 3 minutes, or until soft. Stir in the flour and cook for 1 minute. Stir in the milk, sour cream, chives, lemon juice, salt, pepper, and ½ teaspoon of the lemon peel and cook for 2 minutes, or until slightly thickened.

Divide the ravioli among 4 plates. Spoon the sauce over each serving and top with the cheese and the remaining ½ teaspoon lemon peel.

Makes 4 servings
Per serving: 372 calories, 18 g protein, 34 g carbohydrates, 19 g fat, 64 mg cholesterol, 2 g fiber, 750 mg sodium

---

COOKING TIP

For a change of pace, explore the many flavors of refrigerated fresh ravioli available these days. Try such varieties as four cheese, sausage, and even sun-dried tomato. All will taste great with this sauce.

Rotelle with Escarole and Cannellini

8   ounces tricolor rotelle (corkscrew)
2   tablespoons olive oil
1   onion, chopped
1   carrot, chopped
4   cloves garlic, minced
1   teaspoon Italian seasoning
½   teaspoon salt
8   cups chopped fresh escarole
½   cup vegetable broth
1   can (14–19 ounces) cannellini beans, rinsed and drained

The classic Italian flavors of escarole and cannellini beans are bathed in a light vegetable sauce. Delicious tossed with rotelle.

Prepare the rotelle according to package directions.

Meanwhile, heat the oil in a large saucepan over medium heat. Add the onion, carrot, garlic, Italian seasoning, and salt. Cook, stirring, for 5 minutes, or until the vegetables are tender.

Increase the heat to high. Add the escarole and broth. Cook, stirring, for 2 minutes, or until the escarole is wilted. Add the beans and cook, stirring, for 2 minutes, or until heated through.

Place the rotelle in a serving bowl and top with the escarole mixture.

Makes 4 servings
Per serving: 440 calories, 15 g protein, 76 g carbohydrates, 10 g fat, 0 mg cholesterol, 11 g fiber, 578 mg sodium

Radiatore Ratatouille

1   jar (6 ounces) marinated artichoke hearts
1   onion, chopped
2   cloves garlic, minced
1   tablespoon grated fresh ginger
1   teaspoon ground cumin
1   medium eggplant, peeled and chopped
1   can (14 ounces) stewed tomato
½   cup vegetable broth
½   teaspoon salt
¼   cup chopped fresh cilantro, stems included
8   ounces radiatore or fusilli

Even if you aren't a big fan of eggplant, this dish will have you singing its praises. Simmered with tomatoes and artichoke hearts, the eggplant becomes tender and flavorful.

Drain the artichoke hearts, reserving 2 tablespoons of the marinade. Coarsely chop the artichoke hearts. Set aside.

Heat the reserved oil in a large skillet over medium heat. Add the onion and cook for 5 minutes, or until soft. Add the garlic, ginger, and cumin, and cook, stirring, for 2 minutes. Add the eggplant, tomatoes (with juice), broth, salt, and the reserved artichoke hearts. Bring to a boil over high heat. Reduce the heat to low, cover, and simmer, stirring occasionally, for 5 minutes, or until the eggplant is tender. Stir in the cilantro.

Meanwhile, prepare the radiatore according to package directions.

Place the radiatore in a serving bowl and top with the eggplant mixture.

Makes 4 servings

Per serving: 407 calories, 11 g protein, 63 g carbohydrates, 13 g fat, 0 mg cholesterol, 7 g fiber, 706 mg sodium

Orecchiette with Beans and Broccoli Rabe

8 ounces orecchiette

2 tablespoons olive oil

2 large cloves garlic, minced

1 small red onion, thinly sliced

5 cups coarsely chopped broccoli rabe

½ cup vegetable broth

¼ teaspoon red-pepper flakes

1 tablespoon chopped fresh basil

½ teaspoon salt

1 can (14–19 ounces) small white beans, rinsed and drained

⅓ cup (1½ ounces) shredded Parmesan cheese

Italian for "little ears," orecchiette pasta is shaped like teacup saucers—making it the perfect shape to hold this light sauce. The dish is balanced with broccoli rabe's slightly bitter flavor and mellow white beans.

Prepare the orecchiette according to package directions.

Meanwhile, heat the oil in a large skillet over medium heat. Add the garlic and onion and cook, stirring, for 1 minute, or just until the garlic turns golden. Add the broccoli rabe, broth, red-pepper flakes, basil, and salt. Cook for 2 minutes, or until the broccoli rabe is tender-crisp. Add the beans and cook for 2 minutes, or until heated through.

Add to the orecchiette and toss to combine. Serve topped with the cheese.

Makes 4 servings

Per serving: 583 calories, 27 g protein, 87 g carbohydrates, 15 g fat, 6 mg cholesterol, 11 g fiber, 817 mg sodium

Angel Hair with Roasted Red Pepper Sauce

12 ounces angel hair pasta

2 jars (7 ounces) roasted red peppers, drained

1 tablespoon olive oil

2 tablespoons chopped fresh basil

1 teaspoon sugar

½ teaspoon salt

½ teaspoon freshly ground black pepper

¼ cup (1 ounce) grated Parmesan cheese

No-cook sauces make dinnertime a breeze. Roasted red peppers pack this sauce with flavor that is delicately mellowed with fresh basil.

Prepare the angel hair according to package directions.

Meanwhile, in a food processor or blender, combine the peppers, oil, basil, sugar, salt, and black pepper. Process until smooth.

Place the angel hair in a serving bowl. Add the pepper sauce and toss to coat. Top with the cheese.

Makes 4 servings

Per serving: 390 calories, 11 g protein, 67 g carbohydrates, 8 g fat, 0 mg cholesterol, 3 g fiber, 291 mg sodium

Spinach Pesto Penne

12 ounces penne

1 box (10 ounces) frozen artichoke hearts, thawed

1½ cups packed fresh spinach leaves, stems removed

1 cup packed fresh basil leaves

2 tablespoons olive oil

2 tablespoons water

2 cloves garlic, coarsely chopped

½ teaspoon salt

1 jar (7 ounces) roasted red peppers, drained and chopped

⅓ cup (1½ ounces) crumbled Gorgonzola cheese

This rich green sauce is packed with healthful antioxidants. Spinach adds a nutrient bonus to the garlic-basil pesto.

Prepare the penne according to package directions. Add the artichoke hearts during the last 2 minutes of cooking.

Meanwhile, in a food processor or blender, combine the spinach, basil, oil, water, garlic, and salt. Process until smooth, scraping down the sides of the bowl as necessary.

Place the penne and artichokes in a serving bowl. Top with the pesto, red peppers, and cheese. Toss to coat well.

Makes 4 servings

Per serving: 483 calories, 17 g protein, 72 g carbohydrates, 14 g fat, 15 mg cholesterol, 4 g fiber, 638 mg sodium

COOKING TIP

If you can't find frozen artichoke hearts, use a 15-ounce can of whole artichokes, drained and sliced in half. Add them to the pasta with the pesto.

Rotini with Roasted Vegetables

¼ cup olive oil

2 tablespoons balsamic vinegar

3 cloves garlic, minced

1 teaspoon dried oregano

½ teaspoon salt

½ teaspoon freshly ground black pepper

1 red bell pepper, cut into 1" pieces

1 sweet potato, peeled and cut into ½" pieces

1 small eggplant, peeled and cut into 1" pieces

3 portobello mushrooms, thickly sliced

2 pounds plum tomatoes, halved lengthwise and quartered

1 small head radicchio, coarsely chopped

8 ounces rotini

¼ cup thinly sliced fresh basil

2 tablespoons toasted pine nuts

Roasting vegetables gives them a rich, caramelized flavor. Here, they are tossed with rotini pasta, fresh basil, and pine nuts for a hearty meal.

Preheat the oven to 400°F.

In a large roasting pan, combine the oil, vinegar, garlic, oregano, salt, and black pepper. Add the bell pepper, sweet potato, eggplant, mushrooms, and tomatoes and toss to coat well. Roast for 35 minutes, or until lightly browned and tender. Add the radicchio during the last 10 minutes of roasting.

Meanwhile, prepare the rotini according to package directions.

Place the rotini in a serving bowl. Add the roasted vegetables and any juices and toss to coat well. Top with the basil and pine nuts.

Makes 6 servings

Per serving: 350 calories, 10 g protein, 51 g carbohydrates, 13 g fat, 0 mg cholesterol, 8 g fiber, 132 mg sodium

Quick Lentils and Curried Vegetables

1   **cup couscous**

1   **cup vegetable broth**

1   **can (15 ounces) light coconut milk**

¾   **cup red lentils**

1   **bay leaf**

1   **tablespoon butter**

1   **onion, thinly sliced**

1   **sweet potato, peeled and cut into ¼" cubes**

1   **cup broccoli florets**

8   **ounces mushrooms, sliced**

2   **teaspoons red curry paste**

1   **cup frozen peas**

This dish is the perfect blend of Thai seasonings. The creaminess of the coconut milk cuts the spice of the red curry paste, leaving a wonderful blend of flavors to linger on your tongue.

Prepare the couscous according to package instructions.

Meanwhile, in a 2-quart saucepan over medium-high heat, combine the broth and half of the coconut milk. Bring to a boil over high heat. Add the lentils and bay leaf. Reduce the heat to medium and cook for 15 minutes, or until the lentils are tender. Remove and discard the bay leaf.

Melt the butter in a large skillet over medium heat. Add the onion and sweet potato and cook for 7 minutes, or until the sweet potato is slightly tender.

Add the broccoli and mushrooms and cook for 5 minutes, or until the vegetables are tender. Add the curry paste, peas, lentils, and the remaining coconut milk. Cook for 2 minutes, or until heated through.

Place the couscous in a large bowl and top with the lentil mixture.

Makes 4 servings

Per serving: 501 calories, 23 g protein, 79 g carbohydrates, 12 g fat, 9 mg cholesterol, 18 g fiber, 317 mg sodium

Saffron Orzo with Corn

2 tablespoons olive oil

1 onion, finely chopped

2 cloves garlic, minced

1 cup orzo

1 can (14–16 ounces) black beans, rinsed and drained

2½ cups vegetable broth

½ cup white wine

½ cup frozen corn, thawed

½ cup chopped roasted red peppers

⅛ teaspoon crushed saffron threads or ¹⁄₁₆ teaspoon ground turmeric

¼ cup (1 ounce) shredded provolone cheese

Reminiscent of risotto, this bright yellow orzo studded with dark black beans is a beautiful dish to serve.

Heat the oil in a saucepan over medium heat. Add the onion and garlic and cook, stirring often, for 3 minutes, or until the onion is soft. Add the orzo and cook, stirring constantly, for 2 minutes, or until the orzo is well-coated. Stir in the beans, broth, wine, corn, roasted red peppers, and saffron or turmeric.

Bring to a boil over high heat. Reduce the heat to low, cover, and simmer, stirring occasionally, for 15 minutes, or just until the orzo is tender.

Place in a serving bowl and top with the cheese.

Makes 4 servings

Per serving: 375 calories, 17 g protein, 58 g carbohydrates, 10 g fat, 5 mg cholesterol, 6 g fiber, 1,000 mg sodium

Acini di Peppe with Caramelized Onions

2 tablespoons butter
2 small sweet onions, cut into thin wedges
1 cup acini di peppe
2 tablespoons hoisin sauce
2 tablespoons soy sauce
1 tablespoon honey
¼ teaspoon five-spice powder
2 cups broccoli florets
1 small carrot, shredded
¼ cup (1 ounce) shredded ricotta salata

The secret ingredient in this dish is Chinese five-spice powder. It adds a real flavor boost to the pasta and blends perfectly with the sweet flavor of the caramelized onion.

Melt the butter in a large skillet over medium heat. Add the onions. Cover and cook for 15 minutes, turning once, until golden brown and tender.

Meanwhile, prepare the acini di peppe according to package directions.

In a small bowl, combine the hoisin sauce, soy sauce, honey, and five-spice power.

Remove the onions to a plate. Add the broccoli to the same skillet and cook over medium heat, stirring, for 1 minute. Add the soy sauce mixture and acini di peppe and cook for 4 minutes, or until the broccoli is tender.

Divide the acini di peppe mixture among 4 plates. Top with the onions, carrots, and cheese.

Makes 4 servings

Per serving: 226 calories, 8 g protein, 22 g carbohydrates, 12 g fat, 32 mg cholesterol, 3 g fiber, 786 mg sodium

---

COOKING TIP

Acini di peppe (ah-CHEE-nee dee PAY-pay), Italian for "peppercorns," is tiny pasta in the shape of peppercorns.

Udon Noodles with Broccoli and Peppers

8   ounces udon noodles

2   teaspoons hot chile or toasted sesame oil

2   cups broccoli florets

1   red or green bell pepper, thinly sliced

2   carrots, cut into matchsticks

1   can (8 ounces) sliced water chestnuts, drained

1   cup vegetable broth

2   tablespoons soy sauce

1   tablespoon rice vinegar

2   cloves garlic, crushed

1   tablespoon grated fresh ginger

1   tablespoon cornstarch

These thick Japanese noodles tossed with tender-crisp vegetables are sure to become a favorite. If you can't find udon, spaghetti works well in this dish.

Prepare the noodles according to package directions.

Meanwhile, heat the oil in a large skillet over medium-high heat. Add the broccoli, pepper, carrots, and water chestnuts. Cook, stirring frequently, for 3 minutes, or until the vegetables are tender-crisp.

In a small bowl, whisk together the broth, soy sauce, vinegar, garlic, ginger, and cornstarch. Add to the skillet and cook, stirring constantly, for 2 minutes, or until thickened.

Place the noodles in a serving bowl. Top with the vegetable mixture and toss to coat well.

Makes 6 servings
Per serving: 210 calories, 8 g protein, 42 g carbohydrates, 2 g fat, 0 mg cholesterol, 4 g fiber, 815 mg sodium

Vegetable Lo Mein

8 ounces lo mein noodles

1 tablespoon toasted sesame oil

1 red onion, thinly sliced

3 stalks bok choy, thinly sliced

2 carrots, thinly sliced

½ cup vegetable broth

2 cloves garlic, minced

3 tablespoons soy sauce

2 tablespoons rice vinegar

2 teaspoons cornstarch

4 ounces snow peas, trimmed and sliced lengthwise

This mild dish is a favorite of the teenage set, and it's a great way to get them to eat their vegetables. For a complete meal, add 2 cups of shredded cooked chicken or pork.

Prepare the noodles according to package directions.

Meanwhile, heat the oil in a large skillet over medium-high heat. Add the onion, bok choy, and carrots. Cook for 3 minutes, or until tender-crisp.

In a small bowl, whisk together the broth, garlic, soy sauce, vinegar, and cornstarch, and add it to the skillet. Add the snow peas and cook, stirring constantly, for 3 minutes, or until the sauce is thickened.

Add the noodles and toss to combine. Serve immediately.

Makes 4 servings

Per serving: 183 calories, 7 g protein, 28 g carbohydrates, 5 g fat, 20 mg cholesterol, 4 g fiber, 1208 mg sodium

Sesame Noodles

10 ounces Chinese egg noodles

1 tablespoon peanut oil

3 tablespoons minced fresh ginger

3 scallions, sliced

4 ounces snow peas, trimmed and thinly sliced lengthwise

1 small carrot, shredded

1 cup vegetable broth

3 tablespoons soy sauce

2 teaspoons toasted sesame oil

2 tablespoons rice wine vinegar

⅓ cup creamy peanut butter

¼ cucumber, peeled, seeded, and cut into matchsticks

1 tablespoon toasted sesame seeds

Creamy peanut butter combines with soy sauce and rice wine vinegar for a perfect sauce to coat rich Chinese egg noodles.

Prepare the noodles according to package directions.

Meanwhile, heat the peanut oil in a large skillet over medium-high heat. Add the ginger, scallions, snow peas, and carrot and cook for 1 minute, or until wilted. Remove from the heat. Add the broth, soy sauce, sesame oil, vinegar, and peanut butter. Stir until well-blended.

Place the noodles in a serving bowl. Top with the sauce and toss to coat well. Top with cucumber and sesame seeds. Serve immediately or cover and refrigerate to serve cold.

Makes 4 servings

Per serving: 474 calories, 17 g protein, 64 g carbohydrates, 18 g fat, 0 mg cholesterol, 4 g fiber, 1101 mg sodium

Szechuan Noodles and Bok Choy

- **8** ounces rice sticks (rice-flour noodles)
- **2** tablespoons toasted sesame oil
- **4** stalks bok choy, sliced
- **1** small red pepper, thinly sliced
- **1** tablespoon minced fresh ginger
- **8** asparagus spears, cut into 1" pieces
- **3** scallions, cut diagonally into ½" pieces
- **4** ounces snow peas, trimmed
- **2** cups vegetable broth
- **2** tablespoons soy sauce
- **2** teaspoons garlic-chili sauce

Popular in Asian cooking, garlic-chili sauce can be found in the ethnic aisle of most supermarkets. It adds zest to stir-fried vegetables tossed with noodles.

Prepare the rice sticks according to package directions.

Heat the oil in a large skillet over medium-high heat. Add the bok choy, red pepper, and ginger and cook, stirring, for 3 minutes. Add the asparagus, scallions, snow peas, broth, soy sauce, and garlic-chili sauce. Bring to a boil over high heat. Reduce the heat to low and simmer for 2 minutes, or until the vegetables are tender-crisp.

Add the rice sticks and cook, stirring constantly, for 2 minutes, or until the rice sticks have absorbed most of the liquid.

Makes 4 servings
Per serving: 304 calories, 6 g protein, 58 g carbohydrates, 7 g fat, 0 mg cholesterol, 3 g fiber, 1070 mg sodium

---

COOKING TIP

Rice sticks are about ¼" wide, 6" to 8" long, and made with rice flour. If you can't find them, use rice noodles or a thin Asian noodle.

HEARTY MEAT AND POULTRY ENTRÉES

New Classic Beef Lasagna

1   jar (48 ounces) chunky pasta sauce

2   eggs

2   cups (8 ounces) ricotta cheese

2   cups (8 ounces) shredded smoked mozzarella cheese

2   cloves garlic, minced

½   pound ground beef

10   ounces mushrooms, sliced

8   ounces no-boil lasagna noodles

¼   cup (1 ounce) grated Parmesan cheese

½   cup chopped fresh parsley

The old-fashioned goodness of lasagna gets a new flavor twist from smoked mozzarella. No-boil lasagna noodles and prepared sauce make it a breeze.

Preheat the oven to 375°F. Coat a 13" x 9" baking dish with cooking spray. Pour 2 cups of the sauce in the bottom of the pan.

In a bowl, combine the eggs, ricotta, 1 cup of the mozzarella, and the garlic.

In a large nonstick skillet over medium-high heat, cook the beef and mushrooms, stirring, for 6 minutes, or until the beef is no longer pink. Drain off any fat. Stir in the remaining sauce.

Place a single layer of the lasagna noodles in the bottom of the prepared baking dish. Top with half of the ricotta mixture and a generous 1½ cups of the sauce. Repeat the layering.

Cover with the remaining lasagna noodles, the remaining sauce, and the remaining 1 cup of the mozzarella. Top with the Parmesan and parsley.

Cover with foil and bake for 30 minutes, or until hot and bubbly and the noodles are tender. Remove the foil and bake for 10 minutes. Let stand for 10 minutes before serving.

Makes 12 servings

Per serving: 392 calories, 20 g protein, 34 g carbohydrates, 20 g fat, 88 mg cholesterol, 3 g fiber, 705 mg sodium

Speedy Skillet Macaroni

1 pound ground beef
1 onion, chopped
2 cloves garlic, minced
2 cans (14 ounces each) Mexican-style stewed tomatoes
1 can (14–19 ounces) red kidney beans, rinsed and drained
1 cup elbow macaroni
1 tablespoon taco seasoning
½ cup (2 ounces) shredded Cheddar cheese

This is the perfect meal to make when you are short on time and big on hunger. Your kids will love the great taste of this wholesome one-dish meal, and you will love how easy it is to make.

In a large skillet over medium heat, cook the beef, onion, and garlic, stirring frequently, for 8 minutes, or until the beef is no longer pink. Drain off any fat.

Return the skillet to the heat and stir in the tomatoes (with juice), beans, macaroni, and taco seasoning.

Bring to a boil over high heat. Reduce the heat to low, cover, and simmer, stirring occasionally, for 25 minutes, or until the macaroni is tender. Top with the cheese.

Makes 4 servings

Per serving: 408 calories, 23 g protein, 34 g carbohydrates, 19 g fat, 67 mg cholesterol, 6 g fiber, 537 mg sodium

Beef and Mushroom Penne

8 ounces penne

1 tablespoon olive oil

1 pound sirloin or top-round steak, cut into strips

1 large clove garlic, minced

1 large red onion, cut into thin wedges

8 ounces mixed mushrooms, chopped

½ teaspoon salt

½ teaspoon freshly ground black pepper

1 cup beef broth

½ cup (4 ounces) sour cream

2 tablespoons minced fresh parsley

Mix up your mushrooms! Try combining shiitake, portobello, and crimini with button mushrooms for a real flavor treat. The button mushrooms will pick up the stronger flavors of the exotic mushrooms.

Prepare the penne according to package directions.

Meanwhile, heat the oil in a large nonstick skillet over medium-high heat. Add the steak and garlic and cook, stirring frequently, for 2 minutes, or until the steak is no longer pink. Add the onion, mushrooms, salt, and pepper. Cook, stirring occasionally, for 3 minutes, or until the mushrooms begin to release their juices.

Add the broth and sour cream. Cook, stirring constantly, for 1 minute, or until heated through and slightly thickened. Stir in the parsley.

Place the penne in a serving bowl. Top with the steak mixture.

Makes 6 servings

Per serving: 343 calories, 23 g protein, 32 g carbohydrates, 13 g fat, 52 mg cholesterol, 2 g fiber, 318 mg sodium

Thai-Seasoned Beef and Noodles

8 ounces medium-wide egg noodles

1 tablespoon sesame oil

1 pound sirloin or top-round steak, thinly sliced

2 large tomatoes, coarsely chopped

1 onion, thinly sliced

3 cloves garlic, crushed

2 teaspoons Thai seasoning

1 teaspoon freshly grated ginger

½ cup beef broth

1 tablespoon lime juice

¼ cup chopped fresh mint

2 tablespoons chopped dry roasted peanuts

Thai seasoning is an exotic blend of six or more spices, including lemongrass, cinnamon, and ground red pepper. Along with the lime juice and mint, it gives a lively, fresh flavor to beef and noodles.

Prepare the noodles according to package directions.

Meanwhile, heat the oil in a large skillet over medium-high heat. Add the steak and cook for 3 minutes, or until no longer pink. With a slotted spoon, remove the steak to a plate and keep warm.

Add the tomatoes, onion, garlic, Thai seasoning, and ginger to the same skillet and cook, stirring, for 3 minutes, or until the onion is soft. Stir in the broth and cook for 3 minutes. Stir in the lime juice, mint, and reserved steak.

Place the noodles in a serving bowl. Add the tomato mixture. Toss to coat well and top with the peanuts.

Makes 4 servings
Per serving: 442 calories, 37 g protein, 49 g carbohydrates, 11 g fat, 103 mg cholesterol, 2 g fiber, 293 mg sodium

Spaghetti with Meatballs

2 tablespoons olive oil
2 medium onions, chopped
3 cloves garlic, minced
1 pound ground meatloaf mix (beef, veal, and pork)
⅔ cup seasoned bread crumbs
¼ cup milk
1 egg, lightly beaten
2 teaspoons chopped fresh sage or 1 teaspoon dried
½ teaspoon salt
1 can (28 ounces) whole tomatoes
2 teaspoons Italian seasoning
12 ounces spaghetti

Comfort food doesn't get any better than spaghetti with meatballs. A mix of ground meats creates the most tender, flavorful meatballs.

Heat the oil in a large saucepan over medium heat. Add the onions and garlic and cook, stirring often, for 8 minutes, or until the onions are very soft. Remove ¼ cup of the onion mixture to a large bowl. Set aside the remaining onions.

Preheat the broiler. Coat the broiler pan with cooking spray.

In the bowl with the onions, combine the ground meat, bread crumbs, milk, egg, sage, and salt. Shape into 12 meatballs, about 2" in diameter. Place the meatballs on the prepared pan. Broil, turning occasionally, for 10 minutes, or until browned.

Add the tomatoes (with juice), Italian seasoning, and cooked meatballs to the reserved onions in the saucepan. Bring to a boil over high heat. Reduce the heat to low and cook, breaking up the tomatoes with the back of a spoon, for 25 minutes, or until the meatballs are no longer pink.

Meanwhile, prepare the spaghetti according to package directions.

Place the spaghetti in a serving bowl. Top with the meatballs and sauce.

Makes 6 servings
Per serving: 502 calories, 25 g protein, 64 g carbohydrates, 16 g fat, 98 mg cholesterol, 4 g fiber, 977 mg sodium

Minty Fettuccine with Rosemary Lamb

8   ounces fettuccine

2   cups cauliflower florets

4   ounces fresh spinach

½   cup fresh mint leaves

2   cloves garlic

2   teaspoons lemon peel

2   teaspoons fresh rosemary or 1 teaspoon crushed dried

½   teaspoon salt

½   teaspoon freshly ground black pepper

¼   cup water

2   tablespoons lemon juice

1   pound trimmed boneless lamb steak

½   cup (2 ounces) crumbled feta cheese

Tender lamb accented with a mint-and-rosemary pesto is an easy yet elegant company meal. If you prefer your lamb cooked to medium, increase the broiling time by 1 minute per side.

Prepare the fettucine according to package directions. Add the cauliflower during the last 4 minutes of cooking time.

Meanwhile, preheat the broiler. Coat the broiler pan with cooking spray.

In a food processor or blender, combine the spinach, mint, garlic, lemon peel, rosemary, salt, pepper, water, and lemon juice. Process until smooth.

Spread 2 tablespoons of the spinach mixture over the lamb, coating both sides.

Place the lamb on a broiler-pan rack. Broil for 8 minutes, turning once, or until browned and a thermometer inserted in the center registers 145°F for medium-rare. Place on a cutting board and let stand for 5 minutes.

Place fettuccine and cauliflower on a serving platter. Toss with the remaining spinach mixture. Thinly slice the lamb and place over the fettuccine. Top with the cheese.

Makes 6 servings

Per serving: 398 calories, 35 g protein, 36 g carbohydrates, 12 g fat, 145 mg cholesterol, 7 g fiber, 613 mg sodium

Tex-Mex Bake

8 ounces wagon wheels

2 tablespoons olive oil

1 pork tenderloin (about ¾ pound), cut into ½" slices

1 jar (14–16 ounces) chunky salsa

1 can (14 ounces) Mexican-style stewed tomatoes

1 can (14–19 ounces) black beans, rinsed and drained

1 tablespoon lime juice

1¼ teaspoons ground cumin

½ cup frozen corn kernels, thawed

¾ cup (3 ounces) shredded Monterey Jack cheese

Wagon wheels studded with salsa and pork slices make this a kid-friendly meal. If you don't have pork on hand, this recipe is also perfect with chicken or even ham.

Preheat the oven to 450°F. Coat a 13" x 9" baking dish with cooking spray.

Prepare the wagon wheels according to package directions.

Meanwhile, heat the oil in a large skillet over medium-high heat. Add the pork and cook, stirring often, for 8 minutes, or until no longer pink. Stir in the salsa, tomatoes (with juice), beans, lime juice, and cumin.

Bring to a boil over high heat. Reduce the heat to low, cover, and simmer, stirring occasionally, for 5 minutes. Stir in the corn and wagon wheels.

Place the mixture in the prepared baking dish and sprinkle with the cheese. Bake for 10 minutes, or until hot and bubbly.

Makes 6 servings

Per serving: 349 calories, 24 g protein, 50 g carbohydrates, 12 g fat, 49 mg cholesterol, 6 g fiber, 863 mg sodium

Zesty Tortellini with Sausage

12 ounces spinach and/or cheese tortellini

½ pound bulk sweet Italian sausage

1 red bell pepper, thinly sliced

6 scallions, cut into ½" lengths

½ cup chicken broth

1 tablespoon red wine vinegar

1 tablespoon jalapeño chile pepper jelly

1 teaspoon Italian seasoning

½ cup (2 ounces) shredded Parmesan cheese

¼ cup pine nuts, toasted

Jalapeño chile pepper jelly and wine vinegar combine with chicken broth in this sweet and sour sauce. Tossed with sweet sausage and cheese tortellini, this colorful hearty meal is bursting with flavor.

Prepare the tortellini according to package directions.

Meanwhile, in a large skillet over medium-high heat, cook the sausage for 5 minutes, or until no longer pink. Drain off any fat. Reduce the heat to medium. Add the pepper and scallions and cook, stirring, for 3 minutes, or until the vegetables are just tender.

Add the broth, vinegar, jelly, and Italian seasoning. Cook for 5 minutes, or until the liquid is slightly reduced. Add the tortellini and toss to coat well. Top with the cheese and nuts.

Makes 6 servings

Per serving: 335 calories, 16 g protein, 22 g carbohydrates, 20 g fat, 50 mg cholesterol, 2 g fiber, 696 mg sodium

Shells with Pork and Roasted Vegetables

8 ounces medium shell pasta

½ cup white wine

3 tablespoons frozen orange juice concentrate, thawed

2 tablespoons olive oil

½ teaspoon salt

½ teaspoon freshly ground black pepper

1 pound pork loin, cut into ¾" cubes

3 plum tomatoes, cut in half then quartered

2 large portobello mushrooms, coarsely chopped

2 carrots, cut into ½" pieces

2 small yellow squash, cut in half lengthwise and then into 1" slices

1 tablespoon chopped fresh thyme, or 1 teaspoon dried

1 teaspoon orange peel

Orange juice and white wine blend perfectly to complement the flavors of the pork and summer vegetables. You're sure to get rave reviews for this dish!

Prepare the shells according to package directions.

Meanwhile, preheat the broiler. Coat a 9"x 9" baking dish with cooking spray.

In the baking dish, whisk together the wine, orange juice concentrate, oil, salt, and pepper. Add the pork, tomatoes, mushrooms, carrots, squash, and thyme. Toss to coat well.

Broil, stirring occasionally, for 8 to 10 minutes, or until the vegetables are tender and the pork is no longer pink.

Place the shells in a large serving bowl. Top with the pork mixture and orange peel.

Makes 4 servings
Per serving: 547 calories, 34 g protein, 56 g carbohydrates, 18 g fat, 75 mg cholesterol, 5 g fiber, 391 mg sodium

Hoisin Pork and Vegetables

2 tablespoons hoisin sauce

2 tablespoons soy sauce

1 tablespoon honey

1 tablespoon rice or red wine vinegar

¼ teaspoon crushed red-pepper flakes

1 pork tenderloin (about ¾ pound), cut into ¼" strips

8 ounces udon or soba noodles

1 tablespoon dark sesame oil

6 cups broccoli florets

2 medium carrots, chopped

1 small red or yellow bell pepper

2 cups sliced red or green cabbage

½ red onion, thinly sliced

1 cup chicken broth

The bright bold colors of the carrots, broccoli, and cabbage make this a feast for the eyes. The sweet, saucy flavors are a treat for the tastebuds.

In a small bowl, combine the hoisin sauce, soy sauce, honey, vinegar, pepper flakes, and pork. Toss to coat well and set aside.

Prepare the noodles according to package directions.

Meanwhile, heat the oil in a large skillet over medium heat. Add the broccoli, carrots, pepper, cabbage, and onion and cook, stirring often, for 3 minutes, or until the vegetables just begin to soften. Add the broth, pork, and marinade and cook, stirring, for 5 minutes, or until the pork is no longer pink and the vegetables are tender-crisp.

Place the noodles in a serving bowl. Top with the pork mixture and toss to coat well.

Makes 6 servings
Per serving: 369 calories, 26 g protein, 53 g carbohydrates, 7 g fat, 34 mg cholesterol, 6 g fiber, 897 mg sodium

Smoky Fettuccine Primavera

8 ounces fettuccine

1 tablespoon olive oil

2 cups cauliflower florets

2 carrots, thinly sliced

1 small zucchini, quartered and sliced

1 green bell pepper, chopped

1 red bell pepper, chopped

4 cloves garlic, minced

2 teaspoons fresh rosemary or 1 teaspoon crushed dried

½ pound cooked ham, chopped

¾ cup chicken broth

¾ cup (3 ounces) coarsely grated smoked Gouda cheese

Ham and smoked cheese give this dish a rich, smoky flavor. Tossed with fresh vegetables and fettuccine, this healthy version of fettuccine primavera is sure to please.

Prepare the fettucine according to package directions.

Meanwhile, heat the oil in a large skillet over medium-high heat. Add the cauliflower, carrots, zucchini, bell peppers, garlic, and rosemary. Cook, stirring, for 4 minutes, or until the vegetables are tender-crisp. Add the ham and broth.

Bring to a boil over high heat. Cook for 3 minutes, or until the liquid is slightly reduced.

Place the fettuccine in a serving bowl. Top with the vegetable mixture and the cheese. Toss to coat well.

Makes 4 servings

Per serving: 418 calories, 29 g protein, 43 g carbohydrates, 15 g fat, 113 mg cholesterol, 5 g fiber, 1,081 mg sodium

COOKING TIP

Use a variety of your favorite veggies to personalize this recipe. Try adding asparagus, fresh or frozen peas, fresh cut corn, tomatoes, or even broccoli.

Chicken and Mushroom Rigatoni

8 ounces rigatoni

2 tablespoons butter

1 pound boneless, skinless chicken breasts, cut into 1" strips

1 pound mixed mushrooms (such as porcini, shiitake, and button), sliced

1 shallot, minced

½ teaspoon salt

½ teaspoon freshly ground black pepper

½ cup chicken broth

½ cup dry white wine

½ cup (2 ounces) shredded Asiago cheese

Mushrooms simmered in white wine and tossed with chicken and cheese make this recipe hard to beat. Plus, it's great for casual get-togethers since it can be prepared in less than 30 minutes.

Prepare the rigatoni according to package directions.

Meanwhile, melt 1 tablespoon of the butter in a large skillet over medium-high heat. Add the chicken and cook, stirring often, for 5 to 7 minutes, or until no longer pink. Remove the chicken and set aside.

Melt the remaining 1 tablespoon butter in the skillet. Add the mushrooms, shallot, salt, and pepper and cook, stirring, for 10 minutes, or until the mushrooms release their liquid and it begins to evaporate.

Add the broth and wine and cook for 2 minutes, stirring and scraping up the browned bits on the bottom. Stir in the reserved chicken and rigatoni. Top with the cheese.

Makes 4 servings

Per serving: 496 calories, 41 g protein, 49 g carbohydrates, 13 g fat, 92 mg cholesterol, 2 g fiber, 747 mg sodium

Creamy Chicken and Noodles

8 ounces egg noodles

1 tablespoon olive oil

1 pound boneless, skinless chicken breasts, cut into 1" strips

1 onion, thinly sliced

½ cup orange juice

1 tablespoon grated fresh ginger

1 teaspoon ground cardamom

1 teaspoon ground fennel seeds

¾ cup (6 ounces) sour cream

1 cup milk

Creamy noodles kissed with cardamom and fennel seeds make this chicken dish simply delicious.

Prepare the noodles according to package directions.

Meanwhile, heat the oil in a large skillet over medium heat. Add the chicken and onion and cook, stirring, for 5 minutes, or until browned. Add the orange juice, ginger, cardamom, and fennel seeds. Cook for 3 minutes, or until the chicken is no longer pink and the onion is tender. Stir in the sour cream, milk, and noodles. Toss to coat well.

Serves 4

Per serving: 489 calories, 38 g protein, 51 g carbohydrates, 14 g fat, 139 mg cholesterol, 2 g fiber, 130 mg sodium

---

COOKING TIP

Cardamom is an aromatic spice with a warm, sweet flavor. Related to ginger, it adds a delicate taste to savory and sweet dishes alike.

Southwestern Chicken Lasagna

8 ounces lasagna noodles

2 eggs

1 cup (4 ounces) ricotta cheese

1 can (4.5 ounces) chopped green chile peppers, drained

¼ cup chopped fresh cilantro, stems included

2 cups (8 ounces) grated yellow and white cheese, such as sharp Cheddar and Monterey Jack

1 jar (14–16 ounces) mild chunky salsa

1 can (15 ounces) tomato sauce

4 cups chopped cooked chicken

Make this kid-friendly lasagna for your next fiesta. You can purchase pre-shredded mixed cheese. Look for Mexican or taco varieties to keep with your flavor theme, but any mix of cheese will do.

Preheat the oven to 350°F. Coat a 13" x 9" baking dish with cooking spray.

Prepare the lasagna noodles according to package directions.

Meanwhile, in a large bowl, combine the eggs, ricotta, chile peppers, cilantro, and ½ cup of the shredded cheese.

In a small bowl, combine the salsa and tomato sauce.

Pour 1 cup of the sauce into the prepared baking dish. Spread to cover the bottom. Top with a single layer of lasagna noodles. Top with half of the ricotta mixture, one-third of the chicken, and one-third of the shredded cheese. Top with one-third of the sauce. Repeat the layers.

Cover with the remaining lasagna noodles, the remaining sauce, the remaining chicken, and the remaining shredded cheese.

Cover with foil and bake for 45 minutes, or until hot and bubbly. Remove the foil and bake for 10 minutes. Let stand for 10 minutes before serving.

Makes 12 servings

Per serving: 255 calories, 22 g protein, 19 g carbohydrates, 10 g fat, 112 mg cholesterol, 2 g fiber, 572 mg sodium

Chicken Curry over Couscous

2¼ cups chicken broth

1 cup couscous

1 tablespoon vegetable oil

¾ pound boneless, skinless chicken thighs, cut into 1" pieces

1 sweet potato, peeled and finely chopped

½ cup raisins

1 tablespoon curry powder

1 teaspoon freshly grated ginger

1 small apple, peeled and finely chopped

½ cup frozen peas, thawed

¼ cup finely chopped cilantro

A tart apple, such as a Granny Smith, adds nice flavor to this Indian-inspired dish. To make it even faster, use 2 cups of shredded cooked chicken or turkey.

Bring 1¼ cups of the broth to a boil in a small saucepan over high heat. Remove from the heat and stir in the couscous. Cover and set aside.

Meanwhile, heat the oil in a large skillet over medium-high heat. Add the chicken and cook, stirring frequently, for 5 minutes, or until browned. Stir in the sweet potato, raisins, curry powder, ginger, and remaining 1 cup broth.

Bring to a boil over high heat. Reduce the heat to medium, cover, and simmer, for 10 minutes, or until the potato is tender and the chicken is no longer pink. Add the apple, peas, and cilantro and cook for 3 minutes, or until the peas are cooked.

Fluff the couscous with a fork. Evenly divide the couscous among 4 plates and top with the chicken mixture.

Makes 4 servings

Per serving: 433 calories, 25 g protein, 70 g carbohydrates, 8 g fat, 71 mg cholesterol, 6 g fiber, 428 mg sodium

Apricot Chicken over Penne

8   ounces penne

1   tablespoon olive oil

1   pound boneless, skinless chicken thighs, sliced

1   tablespoon yellow mustard seed

¾   cup chicken broth

¾   cup tangerine-orange juice

¼   cup apricot preserves

¼   cup chopped apricots or golden raisins

1   tablespoon white wine vinegar

¼   cup toasted sliced almonds

1   tablespoon fresh thyme leaves

Fresh thyme not only adds a wonderful flavor to this overall dish but it also adds a nice burst of green color. For a change of pace, fresh basil or cilantro would work nicely.

Prepare the penne according to package directions.

Meanwhile, heat the oil in a skillet over medium-high heat. Add the chicken and mustard seed and cook for 5 minutes, or until brown. Remove the chicken mixture to a plate and keep warm.

Stir in the broth, juice, preserves, apricots or raisins, and vinegar. Bring to a boil over high heat. Reduce the heat to low and simmer, stirring often, for 10 minutes, or until the preserves dissolve and the mixture reduces slightly.

Return the chicken mixture to the skillet and simmer for 5 minutes, or until the chicken is no longer pink.

Place the penne in a serving bowl. Top with the chicken mixture, almonds, and thyme. Toss to coat well.

Makes 4 servings
Per serving: 515 calories, 32 g protein, 66 g carbohydrates, 13 g fat, 94 mg cholesterol, 3 g fiber, 222 mg sodium

Fusilli with Broccoli and Chicken

12 ounces whole wheat fusilli

2 cups small broccoli florets

2 tablespoons olive oil

1 pound boneless, skinless chicken breasts, cut into ¾" cubes

1 small red onion, chopped

1 teaspoon salt

2 tablespoons unbleached all-purpose flour

2 cups milk

½ cup (2 ounces) blue cheese

3 tablespoons chopped fresh dill

This simple, rich cream sauce gets its vibrant flavor from blue cheese and fresh dill.

Prepare the fusilli according to package directions. Add the broccoli during the last 2 minutes of cooking time.

Meanwhile, heat the oil in a large skillet over medium-high heat. Add the chicken, onion, and salt and cook for 8 minutes, or until the chicken is no longer pink. Remove to a bowl and set aside.

In a measuring cup, whisk together the flour and milk. Add to the same skillet and cook, stirring often, over medium heat for 5 minutes, or until the mixture boils and begins to thicken. Add the cheese and dill. Stir until smooth. Stir in the chicken mixture.

Place the fusilli in a serving bowl. Top with the chicken mixture. Toss to coat well.

Makes 4 servings

Per serving: 442 calories, 31 g protein, 51 g carbohydrates, 12 g fat, 62 mg cholesterol, 2 g fiber, 627 mg sodium

COOKING TIP

There are many varieties of blue cheese available these days. Two popular ones are Gorgonzola (made from cow's milk) and Roquefort (made from sheep's milk). The distinctive flavor of all blue cheeses intensifies as it ages. If you prefer a milder flavor, choose a cheese with lighter marbling.

Creamy Rotelle with Chicken

12 ounces tricolor rotelle pasta

2 cups small broccoli florets

2 carrots, thinly sliced

2 tablespoons butter

2 tablespoons unbleached all-purpose flour

2 cups milk

1 cup (4 ounces) shredded Jarlsberg cheese

2 tablespoons dry sherry or wine vinegar

¾ teaspoon freshly ground nutmeg

½ teaspoon salt

3 cups cubed cooked skinless chicken breast (about ¾ pound)

Broccoli and carrots blended in the creamy white sauce make this dish a surefire winner. If you want to add a flavor boost, try a smoked Gouda or Cheddar in place of the Jarlsberg.

Prepare the rotelle according to package directions. Add the broccoli and carrots during the last 4 minutes of cooking time.

Meanwhile, melt the butter in a saucepan over medium heat. Stir in the flour and cook, stirring, for 1 minute. Slowly stir in the milk until smooth. Cook, stirring often, for 5 minutes, or until the mixture boils and thickens. Add the cheese, sherry or vinegar, nutmeg, and salt. Stir until smooth. Add the chicken and cook for 2 minutes, or until heated through.

Place the rotelle and vegetables in a serving bowl. Top with the chicken mixture and toss to coat well.

Makes 6 servings
Per serving: 458 calories, 29 g protein, 52 g carbohydrates, 13 g fat, 65 mg cholesterol, 3 g fiber, 423 mg sodium

Chicken Cacciatore
with Cavatelli

8   ounces cavatelli

2   tablespoons olive oil

1   large onion, chopped

4   cloves garlic, minced

1   can (15 ounces) Italian-style diced tomatoes

6   boneless, skinless chicken thighs (about 1½ pounds)

½   cup whole pitted green or kalamata olives

2   teaspoons fresh rosemary or ¾ teaspoon crushed dried

½   teaspoon salt

While you can use any pitted, whole olives for this recipe, the green olives will add a nice splash of color to your finished dish. If you are using dried rosemary, crush it between your fingers before stirring it in to release its essential oils and enticing aroma.

Prepare the cavatelli according to package directions.

Meanwhile, heat the oil in a large skillet over medium-high heat. Add the onion and garlic and cook for 4 minutes, or until soft.

Stir in the tomatoes (with juice), chicken, olives, rosemary, and salt. Bring to a boil over high heat. Reduce the heat to low, cover, and simmer for 20 minutes, or until the chicken is no longer pink.

Evenly divide the cavatelli among 6 plates. Spoon the chicken mixture over the cavatelli.

Makes 6 servings

Per serving: 362 calories, 29 g protein, 36 g carbohydrates, 11 g fat, 94 mg cholesterol, 3 g fiber, 746 mg sodium

Bow Ties with Chicken and Asparagus

8 ounces bow-tie pasta (farfalle)
1 tablespoon butter
1 onion, thinly sliced
¾ cup chicken broth
½ cup dry white wine
3 cloves garlic, minced
1 tablespoon minced fresh rosemary or 2 teaspoons dried, crushed
¾ pound smoked chicken breast, cut into 2" strips
¾ pound asparagus, ends trimmed, cut into 1½" pieces
½ cup (2 ounces) grated Asiago cheese

Reach for this recipe on those busy weeknights when you need a tasty dinner fast. You can find smoked chicken breast at the deli counter of your supermarket.

Prepare the bow ties according to package directions.

Meanwhile, melt the butter in a large nonstick skillet over medium-high heat. Add the onion and cook, stirring, for 5 minutes, or until very soft.

Add the broth, wine, garlic, and rosemary and cook for 5 minutes, or until the liquid is reduced by half. Add the chicken and asparagus and cook for 5 minutes, or until the chicken is heated through and the asparagus is tender-crisp.

Place the bow ties in a serving bowl. Top with the chicken mixture and the cheese.

Makes 4 servings
Per serving: 324 calories, 37 g protein, 19 g carbohydrates, 9 g fat, 103 mg cholesterol, 4 g fiber, 461 mg sodium

Fusilli with Spinach and Chicken

8 ounces tricolor fusilli

2 tablespoons butter

1 medium onion, chopped

1 tablespoon unbleached all-purpose flour

2½ cups milk

¾ cup (3 ounces) shredded fontina cheese

2 tablespoons Dijon mustard

½ teaspoon salt

½ teaspoon freshly ground black pepper

¾ pound smoked skinless chicken or turkey breast, cut into ½" cubes

1 package (10 ounces) frozen chopped spinach, thawed and squeezed dry

2 tablespoons unseasoned dry bread crumbs

Fusilli and spinach bathed in a cream sauce take comfort food to a new level. Smoked chicken breast and fontina add a rich flavor to this dish.

Preheat the oven to 375°F. Coat an 11" x 7" baking dish with cooking spray.

Prepare the fusilli according to package directions.

Meanwhile, melt the butter in a large saucepan over medium heat. Add the onion and cook, stirring, for 3 minutes, or until soft.

Stir in the flour and cook, stirring, for 1 minute. Slowly stir in the milk until smooth. Cook, stirring often, for 5 minutes, or until the mixture boils and thickens. Add the cheese, mustard, salt, and pepper. Stir until smooth. Add the chicken or turkey, spinach, and fusilli.

Place in the prepared baking dish. Top with the bread crumbs. Bake for 20 minutes, or until hot and bubbly. Let stand for 10 minutes before serving.

Makes 4 servings
Per serving: 590 calories, 40 g protein, 59 g carbohydrates, 21 g fat, 110 mg cholesterol, 4 g fiber, 789 mg sodium

COOKING TIP

There are several types of fontina cheese. Originally from Italy's Fontina Val d'Aosta, Italian fontinas have a creamy texture and a rich, nutty flavor. The American and Dutch varieties are usually more mild.

Radiatore with Fennel Turkey

8 ounces radiatore

1 tablespoon olive oil

1 pound boneless, skinless turkey breast, cut into ½" chunks

3 cloves garlic, minced

½ teaspoon fennel seeds, crushed

½ teaspoon salt

½ teaspoon freshly ground black pepper

2 cans (14 ounces each) stewed tomatoes

1 package (5.2 ounces) Boursin cheese with cracked black pepper

This pasta is shaped like little radiators with ruffled edges and is great for catching the tasty cream sauce. If you can't find the right name on the box, look for a short, chunky pasta—sometimes it goes by the name "ruffles."

Prepare the radiatore according to package directions.

Heat the oil in a large skillet over medium-high heat. Add the turkey, garlic, fennel seeds, salt, and pepper. Cook for 3 minutes, or until the turkey is no longer pink.

Add the tomatoes (with juice). Bring to a boil over high heat. Reduce the heat to low and simmer, stirring frequently, for 10 minutes, or until the sauce has thickened slightly. Add the cheese and cook for 2 minutes, or until melted.

Place the radiatore in a serving bowl. Top with the sauce.

Makes 6 servings

Per serving: 377 calories, 26 g protein, 39 g carbohydrates, 12 g fat, 73 mg cholesterol, 2 g fiber, 592 mg sodium

Turkey Bolognese over Spaghetti

1 tablespoon olive oil
1 pound ground turkey breast
1 medium onion, chopped
1 green bell pepper, chopped
4 cloves garlic, minced
1 tablespoon Italian seasoning
1 teaspoon sugar
½ teaspoon salt
½ cup red wine
1 can (28 ounces) crushed tomatoes
2 tablespoons tomato paste
12 ounces spaghetti

Made with lean turkey breast, this robust sauce makes a perfect weeknight can't-go-wrong meal. It also keeps well, so make a double batch and freeze it for up to 2 months.

Heat the oil in a large saucepan over medium-high heat. Add the turkey, onion, pepper, garlic, Italian seasoning, sugar, and salt. Cook, stirring frequently, for 7 minutes, or until the turkey is no longer pink and the onion and pepper are tender.

Stir in the wine, tomatoes, and tomato paste. Bring to a boil over high heat. Reduce the heat to medium-low and cook, stirring occasionally, for 20 minutes.

Meanwhile, prepare the spaghetti according to package directions.

Evenly divide the spaghetti among 6 plates and top with the sauce.

Makes 6 servings
Per serving: 424 calories, 23 g protein, 57 g carbohydrates, 10 g fat, 60 mg cholesterol, 5 g fiber, 492 mg sodium

Radiatore with Sizzling Turkey and Mango Salsa

8 ounces radiatore

1 mango, chopped

1 can (8 ounces) crushed pineapple in juice, drained, with juice reserved

½ small red onion, finely chopped

1 jalapeño pepper, finely chopped (wear gloves when handling)

½ cup coarsely chopped cilantro

2 tablespoons lime juice

2 tablespoons peanut oil

½ teaspoon salt

½ teaspoon freshly ground black pepper

1 pound turkey breast cutlets, cut into ½" x 2" strips

Delicious hot or cold, this pasta dinner is perfect when you are looking for something light and a little different.

Prepare the radiatore according to package directions.

Meanwhile, in a small bowl, combine the mango, pineapple, onion, jalapeño pepper, cilantro, 1 tablespoon of the lime juice, 1 tablespoon of the oil, ¼ teaspoon of the salt, ¼ teaspoon of the pepper, and 1 tablespoon of the reserved pineapple juice. Set aside.

In a medium bowl, combine the turkey, the remaining 1 tablespoon lime juice, ¼ teaspoon salt, ¼ teaspoon pepper, and the remaining pineapple juice.

Heat the remaining 1 tablespoon oil in a large skillet over medium-high heat. Add the turkey mixture and cook, stirring frequently, for 5 minutes, or until the turkey is no longer pink.

Place the radiatore in a serving bowl. Top with the turkey mixture and mango salsa. Toss to coat well. Serve immediately or refrigerate to serve cold.

Makes 6 servings

Per serving: 339 calories, 28 g protein, 41 g carbohydrates, 6 g fat, 63 mg cholesterol, 2 g fiber, 245 mg sodium

Lasagna Bundles

1 jar (26 ounces) chunky garden tomato sauce

16 lasagna noodles

2 tablespoons olive oil

½ pound ground turkey sausage

1 small eggplant, peeled and chopped

3 cloves garlic, minced

1 container (15 ounces) small curd cottage cheese

2 eggs, lightly beaten

½ cup chopped fresh basil

¾ cup (3 ounces) shredded mozzarella cheese

Here's an elegant way to have lasagna. A sausage-and-cheese filling is spiraled into separate lasagna noodles.

Preheat the oven to 350°F. Spread half the tomato sauce over the bottom of a 13" x 9" baking dish.

Prepare the noodles according to package directions. Drain and arrange noodles in a single layer on a clean work surface to prevent them from sticking together.

Meanwhile, heat the oil in a large nonstick skillet over medium heat. Add the sausage, eggplant, and garlic and cook, stirring frequently, for 8 minutes, or until the sausage is browned and no longer pink.

In a medium bowl, combine the sausage mixture, cottage cheese, eggs, basil, and ¼ cup of the mozzarella.

Spread ⅓ cup of the cheese mixture over the length of each noodle and roll up from one end.

Place the rolls, seam side down, in the prepared baking dish. Top with the remaining sauce and the remaining ½ cup mozzarella.

Cover with foil and bake for 20 minutes, or until hot and bubbly. Remove the foil and bake for 5 minutes.

Makes 8 servings

Per serving: 419 calories, 22 g protein, 47 g carbohydrates, 17 g fat, 80 mg cholesterol, 4 g fiber, 782 mg sodium

Baked Turkey Tetrazzini

8 ounces spaghetti

1 tablespoon olive oil

8 ounces mushrooms, sliced

1 onion, chopped

1 large red bell pepper, chopped

⅓ cup unbleached all-purpose flour

3 cups milk

1 pound cooked turkey breast, cut into ¾" cubes

10 large kalamata olives, sliced

½ cup (2 ounces) grated Parmesan cheese

The perfect make-ahead dinner; prepare this dish to the point of baking, cover, and refrigerate for up to 2 days before baking. For a change of pace, sprinkle the top with seasoned bread crumbs, cracker crumbs, or even crushed potato chips before baking.

Preheat the oven to 350°F. Coat a 3-quart baking dish with cooking spray.

Prepare the spaghetti according to package directions.

Meanwhile, heat the oil in a large skillet over medium-high heat. Add the mushrooms, onion, and pepper and cook for 5 minutes, or until soft.

In a bowl, whisk together the flour and milk. Add the milk mixture to the skillet. Reduce the heat to medium. Cook, stirring constantly, for 5 minutes, or until slightly thickened and bubbling.

Remove from the heat. Add the spaghetti, turkey, olives, and cheese. Toss to coat well. Place in the prepared baking dish.

Cover and bake for 20 minutes. Uncover and bake for 10 minutes longer, or until hot and bubbly. Let stand for 5 minutes before serving.

Makes 6 servings
Per serving: 431 calories, 37 g protein, 43 g carbohydrates, 12 g fat, 84 mg cholesterol, 2 g fiber, 345 mg sodium

Spaghettini Carbonara

8　ounces spaghettini

6　slices turkey bacon, cut into ½" pieces

2　cloves garlic, minced

10　ounces fresh spinach, washed and coarsely chopped

2　eggs

¾　cup milk

¾　cup (3 ounces) grated Romano cheese

½　teaspoon salt

½　teaspoon freshly ground black pepper

The fresh spinach in this dish is a tasty addition to classic carbonara. Don't rush when you make this creamy sauce—be sure to keep the heat low and keep stirring so that you don't end up scrambling the eggs.

Prepare the spaghettini according to package directions.

Meanwhile, cook the bacon in a large skillet over medium heat for 5 minutes, or until crisp. Add the garlic and spinach and cook, stirring, for 3 minutes, or until the spinach is wilted. Remove to a bowl.

In a large bowl, whisk together the eggs, milk, cheese, salt, and pepper. Add to the skillet and cook, whisking constantly, over low heat for 8 minutes, or until thick and creamy. Stir in the bacon mixture.

Place the spaghettini in a serving bowl and toss to coat well.

Makes 4 servings

Per serving: 388 calories, 22 g protein, 47 g carbohydrates, 13 g fat, 144 mg cholesterol, 8 g fiber, 898 mg sodium

SATISFYING SEAFOOD FARE

Spicy Seafood Linguine

12	ounces linguine
1	tablespoon butter
2	shallots, minced
5	large cloves garlic, minced
1	bottle (8 ounces) clam juice
½	cup dry white wine
3	plum tomatoes, chopped
2	tablespoons chopped fresh sage
½	teaspoon red-pepper flakes
18	littleneck clams, scrubbed (see note)
18	mussels, scrubbed and beards removed (see note)

Red-pepper flakes add pizzazz to this fresh tomato sauce, the base for steamed mussels and clams. Be sure to serve with bread to sop up the flavorful sauce.

Prepare the linguine according to package directions.

Meanwhile, melt the butter in a large saucepan over medium-high heat. Add the shallots and garlic and cook, stirring often, for 2 minutes, or until soft. Add the clam juice, wine, tomatoes, sage, and red-pepper flakes. Bring to a boil. Reduce the heat to low, cover, and simmer for 1 minute.

Add the clams and mussels. Cover and simmer for 5 to 10 minutes, or until the clams and mussels open. Discard any unopened clams or mussels.

Place the cooked pasta in a serving bowl. Top with the seafood mixture.

Makes 4 servings

Per serving: 485 calories, 21 g protein, 69 g carbohydrates, 13 g fat, 116 mg cholesterol, 3 g fiber, 297 mg sodium

---

COOKING TIP

To avoid getting grit in your sauce, scrub the clams and mussels under cold running water before you cook them. To remove mussels' beards, simply pull the dark thread out or cut it off.

Linguine with Chili Scallops

12 ounces linguine

2 tablespoons peanut oil

1½ pounds sea scallops

4 large cloves garlic, minced

8 scallions, cut into 1" pieces including green tops

½ cup chili sauce

1½ tablespoons rice wine vinegar

1 tablespoon honey

1 teaspoon ground ginger

½ teaspoon salt

Not only will you love the flavor of the sweet-and-sour accented scallops, you will also be amazed at how something so delicious can be made so quickly.

Prepare the linguine according to package directions.

Meanwhile, heat the oil in a large skillet over medium heat. Add the scallops and garlic and cook for 2 minutes. Stir in the scallions, chili sauce, vinegar, honey, ginger, and salt. Cook, stirring often, for 3 minutes, or until the scallops are opaque.

Place the linguine in a serving bowl. Top with the scallop mixture.

Makes 6 servings

Per serving: 458 calories, 29 g protein, 55 g carbohydrates, 14 g fat, 99 mg cholesterol, 2 g fiber, 934 mg sodium

Angel Hair with Shrimp and Tomato Pesto

12 ounces angel hair

1 cup oil-packed sun-dried tomatoes

1 cup packed fresh basil leaves

2 cloves garlic

¼ cup (1 ounce) grated Romano cheese

1 tablespoon olive oil

1½ pounds medium shrimp, peeled and deveined

1 medium red bell pepper, thinly sliced

3 scallions, thinly sliced

½ teaspoon salt

Make this an easy weeknight meal by preparing the pesto ahead of time. The pesto may be refrigerated, tightly covered, for up to 2 weeks, or frozen for up to 4 months.

Prepare the angel hair according to package directions. Drain, reserving ¼ cup of the pasta water.

Meanwhile, in a food processor or blender, combine the sun-dried tomatoes, basil, garlic, and cheese. Process until smooth. If necessary, add in a tablespoon or two of the pasta cooking water to thin the pesto.

Heat the oil in a large nonstick skillet over medium heat. Add the shrimp, pepper, scallions, and salt. Cook, stirring often, for 4 minutes, or until the shrimp are opaque and cooked through.

Place the angel hair in a large bowl and toss with the pesto. Top with the shrimp mixture.

Makes 6 servings
Per serving: 377 calories, 32 g protein, 39 g carbohydrates, 10 g fat, 239 mg cholesterol, 3 g fiber, 472 mg sodium

Sesame Noodles with Shrimp

8   **ounces soba noodles**

1   **pound medium shrimp, peeled and deveined**

1   **cup chicken or vegetable broth**

2   **tablespoons soy sauce**

2   **tablespoons lime juice**

1   **teaspoon freshly grated ginger**

¼   **teaspoon crushed red-pepper flakes**

2   **tablespoons toasted sesame oil**

1   **teaspoon cornstarch**

3   **scallions, sliced**

1   **carrot, cut into matchsticks**

½   **cup snow peas, trimmed and cut into matchsticks**

1   **tablespoon sesame seeds, toasted**

The dark sesame oil lends a deep, nutty flavor to this Asian-inspired dish. Served hot or cold, this dish is sure to please.

Prepare the soba noodles according to package directions.

Meanwhile, in a large bowl, combine the shrimp, broth, soy sauce, lime juice, ginger, pepper flakes, and 1 tablespoon of the oil. Set aside to marinate for 10 minutes.

Using a slotted spoon, remove the shrimp from the marinade. Place in a small bowl. Stir the cornstarch into the marinade until dissolved.

Heat the remaining 1 tablespoon oil in a large skillet over medium-high heat. Add the shrimp, scallions, and carrot and cook, stirring often, for 2 minutes, or until the shrimp begin to turn pink.

Add the snow peas, cooked noodles, and marinade. Cook for 2 minutes, stirring occasionally, until the shrimp are opaque and cooked through and the sauce is thick.

Sprinkle with the sesame seeds.

Makes 4 servings

Per serving: 514 calories, 38 g protein, 62 g carbohydrates, 14 g fat, 172 mg cholesterol, 4 g fiber, 1,320 mg sodium

---

COOKING TIP

Soba, a thin, brown Japanese noodle, is made from buckwheat and wheat flour. Look for it in the Asian section of your grocery store. Ramen or udon make good substitutes.

Fettuccine Shrimp Primavera

12 ounces fettuccine

2 tablespoons olive oil

3 cloves garlic, minced

2 small zucchini, sliced ¼"
thick

2 plum tomatoes, chopped

½ teaspoon salt

½ teaspoon freshly ground
black pepper

1½ pounds medium shrimp,
peeled and deveined

1 cup frozen peas

2 tablespoons chopped
fresh basil

2 tablespoons lime juice

½ cup (2 ounces) shredded
Asiago cheese

*Crisp vegetables and tender shrimp tossed in a fresh basil-lime
sauce are lovely atop fettuccine.*

Prepare the fettucine according to package directions.

Meanwhile, heat the oil in a large skillet over medium-high
heat. Add the garlic and cook for 1 minute, or just until
golden. Add the zucchini and cook for 2 minutes. Add the
tomatoes, salt, and pepper. Cook for 1 minute.

Stir in the shrimp, peas, basil, and lime juice. Cook, stirring
frequently, for 2 minutes, or until the shrimp are opaque and
cooked through.

Place the fettuccine in a serving bowl. Top with the shrimp
mixture and cheese. Toss to combine.

Makes 6 servings
*Per serving: 416 calories, 36 g protein, 41 g carbohydrates, 12 g fat,
238 mg cholesterol, 4 g fiber, 587 mg sodium*

Creamy Shrimp and Fusilli

8   ounces long fusilli
1   cup chicken broth
1   onion, thinly sliced
2   cloves garlic, minced
1   teaspoon dried thyme
½   teaspoon salt
½   teaspoon freshly ground
     black pepper
1   cup milk
3   tablespoons unbleached
     all-purpose flour
1   pound cooked peeled
     and deveined shrimp
2   cups snow peas,
     trimmed
¼   cup chopped roasted red
     peppers

This rich cream sauce—studded with shrimp and vegetables—bathes long fusilli for an elegant entrée. Made with broth and milk, you get all of the great flavor of traditional cream sauces with a fraction of the fat.

Prepare the fusilli according to package directions.

Meanwhile, in a medium saucepan, combine the broth, onion, garlic, thyme, salt, and black pepper. Bring to a boil over medium-high heat.

In a measuring cup, whisk together the milk and flour until smooth. Whisk into the broth mixture. Reduce the heat to medium and cook, stirring often, for 5 minutes, or until the mixture thickens and begins to boil. Cook, stirring, for 1 minute.

Add the shrimp, snow peas, and roasted red peppers. Cook, stirring, for 3 minutes, or until the shrimp is heated through.

Place the fusilli in a serving bowl and top with the shrimp mixture.

Makes 4 servings

Per serving: 281 calories, 24 g protein, 38 g carbohydrates, 3 g fat, 120 mg cholesterol, 2 g fiber, 610 mg sodium.

Mediterranean Penne

8   ounces penne

2   tablespoons olive oil

1   pound tuna steak, about 1" thick

1   pint (8 ounces) cherry tomatoes, halved

1   pound fresh spinach, trimmed and chopped

2   teaspoons grated lemon peel

½   teaspoon salt

½   teaspoon freshly ground black pepper

½   cup (about 2 ounces) crumbled herb and garlic feta cheese

Garlic- and herb-flavored feta cheese adds a burst of flavor to this dish with minimal work. Tossed with penne, fresh tomatoes, spinach, and tuna, this dish is sure to become a classic.

Prepare the penne according to package directions.

Meanwhile, heat 1 tablespoon of the oil in a large skillet over medium-high heat. Add the tuna and cook for 8 minutes, turning once, or until browned and just opaque.

Remove the tuna to a plate. Cool slightly. Flake with a fork into large pieces.

Heat the remaining 1 tablespoon oil in the same skillet. Add the tomatoes and cook over medium heat for 1 minute. Add the spinach, lemon peel, salt, and pepper. Cook, stirring occasionally, for 3 minutes, or until the spinach just begins to wilt.

Place the penne in a serving bowl. Top with the tuna, spinach mixture, and cheese. Toss to coat well.

Makes 4 servings
Per serving: 495 calories, 39 g protein, 46 g carbohydrates, 17 g fat, 56 mg cholesterol, 12 g fiber, 641 mg sodium.

Cavatelli with Red Clam Sauce

12 ounces cavatelli

2 tablespoons olive oil

1 large red onion, chopped

4 cloves garlic, chopped

1 bottle (8 ounces) clam juice

½ cup white wine

1 can (14 ounces) stewed tomatoes

36 littleneck clams, scrubbed (see note)

1 cup packed fresh sage, chopped

A restaurant favorite, this dish is so simple to prepare that it will become part of your meal repertoire. If you can't find small clams, steam the larger ones separately and add to the sauce just before serving.

Prepare the cavatelli according to package directions.

Meanwhile, heat the oil in a large skillet over medium heat. Add the onion and garlic. Cook, stirring often, for 5 minutes, or until the onion is soft. Stir in the clam juice, wine, and tomatoes (with juice). Bring to a boil over high heat. Reduce the heat to low, cover, and simmer for 10 minutes.

Add the clams and sage. Cook, covered, for 5 minutes, or until the clams open. Discard any unopened clams.

Place the cavatelli in a serving bowl. Top with the clam sauce.

Makes 4 servings

Per serving: 469 calories, 17 g protein, 72 g carbohydrates, 9 g fat, 14 mg cholesterol, 3 g fiber, 558 mg sodium

---

COOKING TIP

Soak the clams to get rid of any grit. Dissolve ⅓ cup salt into 1 gallon water and soak the clams in the solution for an hour. Scrub the clams with a sturdy brush under cold running water after soaking.

Wine-Simmered Monkfish Cavatappi

8   ounces cavatappi

1   tablespoon olive oil

2   red and/or yellow bell peppers, chopped

2   cloves garlic, minced

1   medium bulb fennel, quartered lengthwise and thinly sliced

1   large onion, chopped

1   cup white wine

1   teaspoon fennel seeds, crushed

½   teaspoon salt

1½   pounds monkfish, membrane removed and cut into 4 pieces

Monkfish, often referred to as poor man's lobster, is a wonderfully versatile firm white-flesh fish that is very meaty. The sweet flavor of the fish is heightened when cooked with fennel, peppers, and wine.

Prepare the cavatappi according to package directions.

Meanwhile, heat the oil in a large skillet over medium heat. Add the peppers, garlic, sliced fennel, and onion. Cook, stirring often, for 5 minutes, or until the fennel begins to soften.

Stir in the wine, fennel seeds, and salt. Bring to a boil over high heat. Reduce the heat to low, cover, and simmer for 10 minutes. Add the monkfish. Cook, covered, for 7 to 10 minutes, or until the fish flakes easily and the vegetables are tender.

Evenly divide the pasta among 4 serving bowls. Top each with the fennel mixture and a piece of fish.

Makes 4 servings

Per serving: 458 calories, 33 g protein, 54 g carbohydrates, 7 g fat, 43 mg cholesterol, 5 g fiber, 367 mg sodium

Mafalda with Cajun Catfish

8 ounces short-cut mafalda

2 tablespoons olive oil

2 cloves garlic, minced

1 onion, chopped

1 green bell pepper, finely chopped

1 can (14–16 ounces) diced tomatoes, drained

1 cup chicken broth

1 teaspoon dried oregano

¼ teaspoon ground red pepper

1 cup (8 ounces) sour cream

4 catfish fillets (4 ounces each)

½ teaspoon Cajun seasoning

The ground red pepper on these fillets packs a pleasant little punch. If you don't want any spicy heat, feel free to omit it from the sauce.

Coat a broiler pan with nonstick spray. Preheat the broiler.

Prepare the mafalda according to package directions.

Meanwhile, heat 1 tablespoon of the oil in a large skillet over medium heat. Add the garlic, onion, and bell pepper and cook, stirring often, for 5 minutes, or until soft. Add the tomatoes, broth, oregano, and ground red pepper.

Bring to a boil over high heat. Reduce the heat to low, cover, and simmer for 4 minutes, or until slightly thickened. Remove from the heat and stir in the sour cream and mafalda.

Brush each side of the catfish fillets with the remaining 1 tablespoon oil. Sprinkle the Cajun seasoning over both sides of the catfish. Broil for 6 minutes, turning once, or until the fish flakes easily.

Evenly divide the mafalda mixture among 4 plates. Top each with a catfish fillet.

Makes 4 servings

Per serving: 535 calories, 28 g protein, 53 g carbohydrates, 23 g fat, 74 mg cholesterol, 3 g fiber, 631 mg sodium

Asian Orzo and Shrimp

2	tablespoons soy sauce
2	tablespoons honey
2	tablespoons rice vinegar or lemon juice
3	teaspoons toasted sesame oil
1½	pounds medium shrimp, peeled and deveined
2	cups orzo
1	large red or green bell pepper, thinly sliced
6	scallions, cut into ¾" lengths
3	cloves garlic, minced
2	teaspoons grated fresh ginger

This exotic meal comes together in minutes. In about the amount of time it takes to cook the orzo, you will have dinner on the table and your family cheering for more.

In a medium bowl, combine the soy sauce, honey, vinegar or lemon juice, 2 teaspoons of the oil, and the shrimp. Set aside to marinate for 10 minutes.

Meanwhile, prepare the orzo according to package directions.

Using a slotted spoon, remove the shrimp from the marinade. Place in a small bowl. Reserve the marinade.

Heat the remaining 1 teaspoon oil in a large nonstick skillet over medium-high heat. Add the shrimp, pepper, scallions, garlic, and ginger. Cook, stirring frequently, for 3 minutes. Stir in the orzo and the reserved marinade. Cook for 2 minutes, or until the shrimp are opaque and cooked through.

Makes 6 servings
Per serving: 440 calories, 33 g protein, 64 g carbohydrates, 5 g fat, 172 mg cholesterol, 1 g fiber, 514 mg sodium

Easy Salmon and Rotini Casserole

8 ounces rotini

1½ cups each broccoli and cauliflower florets

1 rib celery, thinly sliced

1 small onion, finely chopped

2 tablespoons butter

2 tablespoons unbleached all-purpose flour

1½ cups milk

¾ cup (3 ounces) shredded Cheddar cheese

¾ teaspoon dried marjoram

1 can (7 ounces) skinless, boneless salmon, drained and flaked

2 tablespoons seasoned dry bread crumbs

The best thing about this dish is that you probably have the ingredients in your pantry! In a pinch, use pre-cut broccoli and cauliflower from your grocer's salad bar.

Preheat the oven to 350°F. Coat an 11" x 7" baking dish with cooking spray.

Prepare the rotini according to package directions. Add the broccoli and cauliflower, celery, and onion during the last 5 minutes of cooking.

Meanwhile, melt the butter in a large saucepan over medium heat. Stir in the flour and cook, stirring, for 1 minute, or until the flour is lightly browned. Stir in the milk until smooth. Cook, stirring often, for 5 minutes, or until thickened.

Remove from the heat. Stir in the cheese and marjoram. Continue stirring until the cheese is melted and the mixture smooth. Gently stir in the salmon and pasta mixture.

Pour into the prepared baking dish. Top with the bread crumbs. Bake for 25 minutes, or until hot and bubbly.

Makes 6 servings

Per serving: 343 calories, 16 g protein, 38 g carbohydrates, 14 g fat, 40 mg cholesterol, 2 g fiber, 343 mg sodium

Smoked Salmon with Creamy Dill Linguine

- **8** ounces linguine
- **½** pound asparagus, trimmed and cut into 1½" pieces
- **¾** cup (6 ounces) sour cream
- **½** cup milk
- **1** tablespoon white wine vinegar
- **2** tablespoons chopped fresh dill
- **½** teaspoon salt
- **½** teaspoon freshly ground black pepper
- **1½** cups halved yellow or red cherry tomatoes
- **1** package (3 ounces) smoked salmon, cut into thin strips

Smoked salmon paired with fresh dill in a creamy sauce makes this dinner hard to beat. Enjoy it in the height of summer when the tomatoes are bursting with flavor.

Prepare the linguine according to package directions. Add the asparagus during the last 30 seconds of cooking.

Meanwhile, in a large bowl, whisk together the sour cream, milk, vinegar, dill, salt, and pepper. Add the tomatoes, salmon, and pasta mixture. Toss to coat well.

Makes 4 servings
Per serving: 318 calories, 15 g protein, 39 g carbohydrates, 12 g fat, 88 mg cholesterol, 3 g fiber, 519 mg sodium

Ziti with Rosemary Swordfish

8   ounces ziti

2   tablespoons olive oil

1   pound swordfish, cut into
     1" cubes

3   cloves garlic, crushed

1   teaspoon dried rosemary,
     crushed

½   teaspoon salt

½   teaspoon freshly ground
     black pepper

1   onion, chopped

1   can (14½ ounces)
     stewed tomatoes

1   zucchini, halved
     lengthwise and sliced ¼"
     thick

½   cup chicken broth

2   tablespoons orange juice

Swordfish is the perfect choice for this dish because it doesn't fall apart when you cook it. Enjoy it here with a touch of orange and hint of rosemary.

Prepare the ziti according to package directions.

Heat 1 tablespoon of the oil in a large skillet over medium-high heat. Add the swordfish, garlic, rosemary, salt, and pepper. Cook, stirring occasionally, for 4 minutes, or until the swordfish is opaque. Remove to a plate and keep warm.

Add the remaining 1 tablespoon oil to the same skillet. Add the onion and cook for 3 minutes, or until soft. Add the tomatoes (with juice), zucchini, broth, and orange juice.

Bring to a boil over high heat. Reduce the heat to low, cover, and simmer for 5 minutes, or until the zucchini is just tender. Stir in the swordfish.

Place the ziti in a serving bowl. Top with the swordfish mixture.

Makes 4 servings

Per serving: 664 calories, 46 g protein, 77 g carbohydrates, 18 g fat, 93 mg cholesterol, 4 g fiber, 941 mg sodium

FAST-FIXING MACARONI SALADS

Easy Macaroni Salad

8   ounces elbow macaroni
4   ribs celery, sliced
3   scallions, sliced
½   cup frozen peas, thawed
1   jar (7 ounces) roasted red peppers, drained and finely chopped
2   hard-cooked eggs, coarsely chopped
½   cup (4 ounces) sour cream
½   cup mayonnaise
3   tablespoons cider vinegar
½   teaspoon salt
½   teaspoon white pepper

Planning a picnic or barbecue? This salad is perfect to prepare a day ahead of time. By using sour cream and mayonnaise for the dressing, you get all the creaminess of macaroni salad without all the fat.

Prepare the macaroni according to package directions. Rinse under cold water and drain.

Meanwhile, in a large bowl, combine the celery, scallions, peas, roasted peppers, eggs, sour cream, mayonnaise, vinegar, salt, and pepper. Add the macaroni. Toss to coat well.

Serve immediately or refrigerate for up to 24 hours.

Makes 8 servings
Per serving: 273 calories, 7 g protein, 27 g carbohydrates, 16 g fat, 66 mg cholesterol, 2 g fiber, 276 mg sodium

Penne with Spring Vegetables

8   ounces penne

1   cup baby carrots

6   spears asparagus, cut into 1" pieces

1   cup sugar snap peas, trimmed

4   scallions, cut into 1" pieces

1   plum tomato, cut into wedges

1   cup rinsed and drained canned kidney beans

2   tablespoons capers, drained

¾   cup Italian dressing

½   cup (2 ounces) shredded Parmesan cheese

Here, simple ingredients combine to make one delicious pasta salad. If you don't care for kidney beans, feel free to use small white beans or chickpeas instead.

Prepare the penne according to package directions. Add the baby carrots during the last 2 minutes of cooking. Add the asparagus and snap peas during the last 30 seconds of cooking. Rinse the cooked penne and vegetables under cold water and drain.

In a serving bowl, combine the penne and vegetables with the scallions, tomato, beans, capers, dressing, and cheese. Toss to coat well.

Serve immediately or refrigerate for up to 24 hours.

Makes 6 servings

Per serving: 387 calories, 13 g protein, 46 g carbohydrates, 18 g fat, 7 mg cholesterol, 6 g fiber, 588 mg sodium

Summery Pasta Salad

8   ounces rotelle

3   tablespoons extra-virgin olive oil

2   tablespoons fresh lime juice

2   teaspoons Dijon mustard

1   clove garlic, minced

1   teaspoon ground cumin

½   teaspoon salt

½   teaspoon freshly ground black pepper

3   plum tomatoes, chopped

3   scallions, thinly sliced

1   small green pepper, chopped

1   can (15 ounces) dark red kidney beans, rinsed and drained

1   cup frozen corn, thawed

1   cup (4 ounces) shredded sharp Cheddar cheese

¼   cup sliced kalamata olives

Loaded with vegetables and beans, this hearty salad works as a meal in itself. It's also wonderfully versatile, so feel free to vary the pasta, beans, and vegetables.

Prepare the rotelle according to package directions. Drain and rinse under cold water.

Meanwhile, in a serving bowl, combine the oil, lime juice, mustard, garlic, cumin, salt, and black pepper. Add the tomatoes, scallions, green pepper, beans, corn, cheese, olives, and rotelle. Toss to coat well.

Serve immediately or refrigerate for up to 24 hours.

Makes 8 servings
Per serving: 288 calories, 11 g protein, 37 g carbohydrates, 10 g fat, 15 mg cholesterol, 5 g fiber, 374 mg sodium

Tomato and Fusilli Salad with Feta Dressing

8 ounces tricolor fusilli or rotini

½ cup (2 ounces) feta cheese, crumbled

⅓ cup (2½ ounces) plain yogurt

⅓ cup mayonnaise

1 tablespoon lemon juice

2 tablespoons fresh chopped mint or 2 teaspoons dried

2 cloves garlic, chopped

6 cups chopped arugula or watercress

2 cups halved cherry tomatoes

¾ cup raisins

The flavors of the Mediterranean abound in this fresh salad. Peppery arugula combined with feta and mint are sure to win rave reviews.

Prepare the fusilli according to package directions. Rinse under cold water and drain.

Meanwhile, in a food processor or blender, combine the cheese, yogurt, mayonnaise, lemon juice, mint, and garlic. Process until smooth.

In a serving bowl, combine the arugula, tomatoes, raisins, and fusilli. Top with the dressing and toss to coat well.

Serve immediately.

Makes 4 servings

Per serving: 428 calories, 12 g protein, 50 g carbohydrates, 22 g fat, 38 mg cholesterol, 4 g fiber, 455 mg sodium

Tortellini and Broccoli Salad

1   **package (16 ounces) cheese- or meat-filled tortellini**

3   **cups broccoli florets**

¼   **cup olive oil**

2   **tablespoons red wine vinegar**

1   **tablespoon coarse grain mustard**

2   **cloves garlic, minced**

2   **teaspoons honey**

2   **teaspoons dried basil**

½   **teaspoon salt**

1   **small red onion, chopped**

4   **scallions, sliced ½" thick**

½   **pint cherry tomatoes, halved**

¾   **cup (3 ounces) shredded Romano cheese**

Tortellini makes a wonderful cold salad when tossed with fresh vegetables and a robust vinaigrette.

Prepare the tortellini according to package directions. Add the broccoli during the last 3 minutes of cooking. Rinse under cold water and drain.

In a large bowl, whisk together the oil, vinegar, mustard, garlic, honey, basil, and salt. Add the tortellini, broccoli, onion, scallions, tomatoes, and cheese. Toss to coat well.

Serve immediately or refrigerate for up to 24 hours.

Makes 6 servings
Per serving: 273 calories, 10 g protein, 24 g carbohydrates, 15 g fat, 19 mg cholesterol, 3 g fiber, 515 mg sodium

Warm Turkey and Gemelli Salad

8 ounces gemelli or penne
2 tablespoons olive oil
1 pound boneless, skinless turkey breasts, cut into 1" strips
1 yellow summer squash, cut into thin 2" lengthwise strips
1 green bell pepper, chopped
1 large clove garlic, minced
½ cup chicken broth
¼ cup balsamic vinegar
1 tablespoon Dijon mustard
½ teaspoon salt
½ teaspoon freshly ground black pepper
4 cups mixed salad greens or mesclun

Turkey strips tossed with summer vegetables and gemelli are delicious when laced with a balsamic sauce. This colorful mixture makes a hearty meal over a bed of salad greens.

Prepare the gemelli or penne according to package directions.

Meanwhile, heat the oil in a large skillet over medium-high heat. Add the turkey and cook, stirring, for 5 minutes, or until lightly browned.

Add the squash, bell pepper, and garlic and cook, stirring occasionally, for 5 minutes, or until the vegetables are just tender. Place in a large bowl with the pasta.

Add the broth, vinegar, mustard, salt, and black pepper to the same skillet. Bring to a boil over high heat. Cook, scraping up any browned bits, for 1 minute, or until slightly reduced. Pour over the gemelli mixture.

Evenly divide the salad among 6 plates. Top with the gemelli mixture and serve immediately.

Makes 6 servings
Per serving: 324 calories, 29 g protein, 37 g carbohydrates, 6 g fat, 63 mg cholesterol, 3 g fiber, 304 mg sodium

Ditalini and White Bean Salad

8   ounces ditalini

3   tablespoons olive oil

2   tablespoons lemon juice

2   tablespoons balsamic or red wine vinegar

1   tablespoon Dijon mustard

1   tablespoon chopped fresh thyme or sage or 1 teaspoon dried

½   teaspoon salt

½   teaspoon freshly ground black pepper

1   can (14–19 ounces) white beans, rinsed and drained

6   scallions, sliced

1   red bell pepper, chopped

Pair this salad with grilled chicken or burgers to round out any meal. The Dijon mustard and fresh herbs complement the beans and pasta, making this a great flavor combination.

Prepare the ditalini according to package directions. Rinse under cold water and drain.

In a serving bowl, whisk together the oil, lemon juice, vinegar, mustard, thyme or sage, salt, and black pepper. Add the beans, scallions, bell pepper, and ditalini. Toss to coat well.

Serve immediately or refrigerate for up to 24 hours.

Makes 6 servings

Per serving: 307 calories, 11 g protein, 48 g carbohydrates, 8 g fat, 0 mg cholesterol, 6 g fiber, 384 mg sodium

Orange Couscous Salad

¾ cup couscous

2 tablespoons frozen orange juice concentrate

1 tablespoon fresh oregano or 1 teaspoon dried

1 teaspoon grated orange peel

½ teaspoon salt

¼ teaspoon freshly ground black pepper

1 cup boiling water

1 can (11½ ounces) mandarin orange slices, drained

2 scallions, thinly sliced

½ cup chopped fresh parsley

¼ cup pitted and sliced kalamata olives

1 tablespoon olive oil

Olives, oregano, and orange combine to make a light, fresh dressing for delicate couscous.

In a large bowl, combine the couscous, orange juice concentrate, oregano, orange peel, salt, and pepper. Stir in the water. Cover and let stand for 5 minutes, or until the liquid has been absorbed.

Fluff with a fork. Add the oranges, scallions, parsley, olives, and oil. Toss to coat well. Serve immediately.

Makes 4 servings
Per serving: 231 calories, 5 g protein, 38 g carbohydrates, 6 g fat, 0 mg cholesterol, 2 g fiber, 413 mg sodium

Couscous with Almonds and Apricots

1 tablespoon olive oil

1 small sweet potato, peeled and chopped

1 small red bell pepper, chopped

½ teaspoon ground cinnamon

¼ teaspoon freshly ground nutmeg

¼ teaspoon salt

1 cup apple juice

1 cup couscous

⅓ cup chopped dried apricots

¼ cup sliced almonds

¼ cup lemon juice

Using apple juice instead of water to make the couscous gives this salad a pleasantly sweet flavor your whole family will love. Try it tonight with roasted chicken!

Heat the oil in a large skillet over medium heat. Add the sweet potato, pepper, cinnamon, nutmeg, and salt. Cook, stirring, for 4 minutes, or until the vegetables are soft. Add the apple juice. Bring to a boil over high heat. Stir in the couscous and apricots. Remove from the heat. Cover and let stand for 5 minutes.

Place in a serving bowl. Add the almonds and lemon juice. Toss to coat well. Serve immediately.

Makes 4 servings

Per serving: 339 calories, 9 g protein, 60 g carbohydrates, 8 g fat, 0 mg cholesterol, 6 g fiber, 157 mg sodium

Wilted Spinach-Bacon Salad with Bow Ties

12 ounces bow-tie pasta (farfalle)

2 tablespoons olive oil

4 ounces sliced Canadian bacon, cut into thin strips

4 shallots, thinly sliced

1 teaspoon herbs de Provence

1 pound baby spinach or escarole, coarsely chopped

1 ripe Bartlett pear, quartered, cored, and thinly sliced

½ teaspoon salt

½ teaspoon freshly ground black pepper

1 can (14–19 ounces) cannellini beans, rinsed and drained

2 tablespoons balsamic vinegar

6 ounces goat cheese, crumbled

This elegant salad makes a lovely lunch or light dinner. Serve with crusty bread and white wine for a simple yet satisfying meal.

Prepare the bow ties according to package directions. Lightly rinse under cold water and drain.

Meanwhile, heat the oil in a large skillet over medium-high heat. Add the bacon, shallots, and herbs de Provence and cook for 2 minutes, or until the bacon is lightly browned. Stir in the spinach, pear, salt, and pepper. Reduce the heat to medium and cook, stirring, for 2 minutes, or just until the spinach is wilted.

In a large bowl, combine the bow ties, bacon mixture, beans, and vinegar. Toss to combine. Evenly divide among 6 plates. Top with the goat cheese. Serve immediately.

Makes 6 servings

Per serving: 486 calories, 25 g protein, 66 g carbohydrates, 13 g fat, 24 mg cholesterol, 12 g fiber, 852 mg sodium

---

COOKING TIP

Herbs de Provence—a blend of rosemary, sage, basil, fennel seed, thyme, lavender, and marjoram—can be found in the spice section of most supermarkets.

Index

Boldface references indicate photographs.

CONVERSION CHART

These equivalents have been slightly rounded to make measuring easier.

VOLUME MEASUREMENTS

U.S.	Imperial	Metric
¼ tsp	–	1 ml
½ tsp	–	2 ml
1 tsp	–	5 ml
1 Tbsp	–	15 ml
2 Tbsp (1 oz)	1 fl oz	30 ml
¼ cup (2 oz)	2 fl oz	60 ml
⅓ cup (3 oz)	3 fl oz	80 ml
½ cup (4 oz)	4 fl oz	120 ml
⅔ cup (5 oz)	5 fl oz	160 ml
¾ cup (6 oz)	6 fl oz	180 ml
1 cup (8 oz)	8 fl oz	240 ml

WEIGHT MEASUREMENTS

U.S.	Metric
1 oz	30 g
2 oz	60 g
4 oz (¼ lb)	115 g
5 oz (⅓ lb)	145 g
6 oz	170 g
7 oz	200 g
8 oz (½ lb)	230 g
10 oz	285 g
12 oz (¾ lb)	340 g
14 oz	400 g
16 oz (1 lb)	455 g
2.2 lb	1 kg

LENGTH MEASUREMENTS

U.S.	Metric
¼"	0.6 cm
½"	1.25 cm
1"	2.5 cm
2"	5 cm
4"	11 cm
6"	15 cm
8"	20 cm
10"	25 cm
12" (1')	30 cm

PAN SIZES

U.S.	Metric
8" cake pan	20 × 4 cm sandwich or cake tin
9" cake pan	23 × 3.5 cm sandwich or cake tin
11" × 7" baking pan	28 × 18 cm baking tin
13" × 9" baking pan	32.5 × 23 cm baking tin
15" × 10" baking pan	38 × 25.5 cm baking tin (Swiss roll tin)
1½ qt baking dish	1.5 liter baking dish
2 qt baking dish	2 liter baking dish
2 qt rectangular baking dish	30 × 19 cm baking dish
9" pie plate	22 × 4 or 23 × 4 cm pie plate
7" or 8" springform pan	18 or 20 cm springform or loose-bottom cake tin
9" × 5" loaf pan	23 × 13 cm or 2 lb narrow loaf tin or pâté tin

TEMPERATURES

Fahrenheit	Centigrade	Gas
140°	60°	–
160°	70°	–
180°	80°	–
225°	105°	¼
250°	120°	½
275°	135°	1
300°	150°	2
325°	160°	3
350°	180°	4
375°	190°	5
400°	200°	6
425°	220°	7
450°	230°	8
475°	245°	9
500°	260°	–